RED POWER
The American Indians'
Fight for Freedom

OTHER BOOKS ON AMERICAN INDIANS BY
ALVIN M. JOSEPHY, JR.

THE PATRIOT CHIEFS
THE NEZ PERCE INDIANS AND
THE OPENING OF THE NORTHWEST
THE INDIAN HERITAGE OF AMERICA
Editor
THE AMERICAN HERITAGE
BOOK OF INDIANS

RED POWER
The American Indians' Fight for Freedom

ALVIN M. JOSEPHY, Jr.

AMERICAN HERITAGE PRESS
New York

The author makes grateful acknowledgment for permission to reprint the following material:

"Indian Self-Government," by Felix S. Cohen, in *The Legal Conscience: Selected Papers of Felix S. Cohen,* edited by Lucy Kramer Cohen. © 1970 by Yale University Press. Reprinted by permission.

"This Country Was a Lot Better Off When the Indians Were Running It," by Vine Deloria, Jr. *The New York Times Magazine,* March 8, 1970. © 1970 by The New York Times Company. Reprinted by permission.

Our Brother's Keeper: The Indian in White America, edited by Edgar S. Cahn. © 1969 by The New Community Press. Excerpt reprinted by permission.

TO THE AMERICAN INDIANS
AND ALL THEIR TRUE ALLIES

CONTENTS

Once we were happy in our own country and we were seldom hungry, for then the two-leggeds and the four-leggeds lived together like relatives, and there was plenty for them and for us. But the Wasichus [white men] came, and they have made little islands for us and other little islands for the four-leggeds, and always these islands are becoming smaller, for around them surges the gnawing flood of the Wasichu; and it is dirty with lies and greed.

Black Elk, a Holy Man of the Oglala Sioux

THE NEW INDIAN PATRIOTS

An Introduction by Alvin M. Josephy, Jr.

In 1964 some patronizing whites, wealthy do-gooders of the kind that had long been satisfying their own frustrations and problems by asserting possessory rights over American Indians—"protecting" them against other whites, solving their problems for them, and in their arrogance treating the Indians as children who could have no idea what was best for them in this best of all possible worlds—got the shock of their lives.

As they had done many times before, they took a group of Indians to New York to meet the press and other makers of public opinion in the eastern fountainhead of American communications so that the Indians could tell them, once again, of the problems on the reservations. This time a bolt of lightning struck.

The Indians were young, college-educated, articulate—and fed up. They represented a new organization of their own, the National Indian Youth Council, and they had a lot to say. To the consternation of their patrons, and to the delight of the open-mouthed and unbelieving press, they attacked the do-gooders and told them to get off the Indians' backs; they ridiculed their own elders, the "Uncle Tomahawks" among the tribal leaders, who for decades had sold out the Indians by letting the do-gooders decide what was best for their people; and they demanded Red Power—power of the Indian people over all their own affairs.

Those young Indians, those who came to New York and those whom they represented (and their names are already a part of history: Clyde Warrior, a Ponca; Melvin Thom, a Nevada Paiute; Herbert Blatchford, a Navajo; Bruce Wilkie, a Makah from Washington State; and others) started something. They had cast off dependence on their conquerors and oppressors; they had looked inward at the values and strengths of their own peoples; and they had sounded a call for all Indians to use those strengths to establish lives for themselves on their own terms.

The slogan "Red Power" was articulated at first partly with tongue in cheek. Borrowed from "Black Power," with which black militants were already moving both blacks and whites to face each other in idea-shattering confrontations, it had an initial shock value on just the persons whom it should have shocked. The patronizers were angered by the ingratitude of their "wards" (never ones to feel particularly friendly to blacks, the do-gooders revealed their racism with such reactions as "the Indians are behaving just like the blacks"). The oppressed and desperate Indians on the reservations and the lonely and anxious ones in the cities and at white men's educational institutions sat up, took notice, and began to put pressure on the "Uncle Tomahawks" who had abdicated their responsibilities and loyalties to their peoples. And the rest of the population, with pleasure or fear—depending on their attitudes about the rights of minorities—cheered the Indians' new fighting spirit or fulminated against "Red Muslims" who were urging a race war against the whites. It took no time at all for the humor to drop away and for the coiners of the slogan, and of its equivalent, "Indian Power," to see that they had given voice to a new, and totally serious, idea and force.

Red Power, as it has been taken up in the intervening years by Indians throughout the United States (as well as in Canada), today reflects a determined and patriotic Indian fight for freedom—freedom from injustice and bondage, freedom from patronization and oppression, freedom from what the white man cannot and will not solve.

The background of this American Indian revolution—for it must be viewed as such—has been stated many times, but it is the setting for the struggle, and it should be reiterated here.

For almost five hundred years Indians have been fighting defensively for their right to exist—for their freedom, their lands, their means of livelihood, their organizations and societies, their beliefs, their ways of life, their personal security, their very lives. Those who still remain after so many generations of physical and cultural genocide continue to be oppressed by shattering problems, most of them created by the intruder, conqueror, and dispossessor—the white man.

In the United States of the 1970's, Indian Americans are the poorest of the poor:

Their average life expectancy is 63.9 years; for all other Americans, it is 70;

Their average annual income, $1,500, is 75 per cent less than the national average, and $1,000 below that of the average black family;

Their unemployment rate is nearly 40 per cent, about ten times the national average;

Fifty thousand Indian families live in grossly substandard houses, many without running water, electricity, or adequate sanitary facilities;

Their infant mortality after the first month of life is three times the national average;

Fifty per cent of Indian schoolchildren—double the national average—drop out, or more properly stated, are pushed out by inadequate educational systems before they complete high school;

The suicide rate of Indian teen-agers is one hundred times that of whites (how telling is this statement, reduced to a cold, impersonal statistic that conveys nothing of the human pressures and sufferings!).

However, for the approximately 800,000 Indian Americans —more than 460,000 of them dwelling on or near reservations—these data are only a part of the travail, the portion that protrudes above the water like the tip of an iceberg. The social statisticians observe these figures and conclude that they represent "the problems to be solved."

What lies below the surface, the much larger base and cause of the problems of existence, is the mass of injustices that continue to deny to Indians their rights, desires, and abilities to build viable societies for themselves. The Indians are aware of this base of their problems; the white men, by and large, are ignorant of it.

Ever since the white man reached the New World, he has recognized "Indian problems" (though usually not recognizing that he created them himself) and has tried an unending variety of methods to solve them. The methods have had one goal in common: solution, to the white man, meant forcing the Indian into the mainstream of the dominant culture's way of life — in short, turning the Indian into a white. Inevitably, all programs and policies were defeated by having two built-in defects. First, they took no account of a background of up to twenty-five thousand years of Indian histories and cultures that had nothing in common with the European-based cultures of the white man and could not be shed at the white man's command. And second, the solutions were those of the whites, not of the Indians. The white man, rarely understanding the people whose problems he was trying to solve, imposed his ideas of proper solutions on the Indians, who either could not or would not accept them, and the programs failed.

The Indian was never silent. He spoke out, trying to tell the white man what his people needed and what they could accept. But the whites, with few exceptions, never listened. In their minds the Indians were stereotypes — savages, children, wards — inferior to civilized peoples; they were therefore unable to know what was good for them and were utterly devoid of the wisdom or ability to plan and manage their own affairs. Tragedy was thus heaped on tragedy. When physical genocide slackened, cultural genocide — the enforced ending of Indian cultures, life styles, organizations, and values and thinking, of "Indianness" itself — took over, with the misguided belief that the persistence of such remnants of the past perpetuated the Indians' difficulties. Land, dignity, and the means of existence were all robbed by despoilers and free-booters, encouraged by missionaries, army officers, and government agents intent on ridding the nation of Indian life and content.

Today, for the first time in the United States, that approach is beginning to change. It is still widely held by the unknowing that so long as Indians insist on being Indians and maintaining their reservations as the basis of their life, just so long will they sit in poverty and indolence and starve. But the ranks of the more knowledgeable among non-Indians are growing. Attracted first to the struggle of the blacks, Americans have become seriously attentive to the status and needs of all minorities within the nation. The resulting new interest in Indians has created a climate for an increase in realistic understanding of what the Indians have been saying.

It must also be understood that the Indians themselves have helped in creating this new climate. Increasing numbers of Indians are learning how to communicate with non-Indians so that the latter will listen and understand. Indian organizations are becoming stronger and more practiced in their use of the non-Indians' communications media, and together with the individual tribes and their leaders, and with Indian scholars and intellectuals, they are riding the winds of change that are abroad in today's world, demanding and receiving the attention of the non-Indians.

In the new climate the strongest and loudest Indian voices are those that speak selflessly and patriotically of Red — or Indian — Power. Their numbers are swelling, particularly among the younger Indians. In substance their message is no different from what it has been for decades, but it is more challenging and insistent. It demands, rather than pleads for, self-determination: the right of Indians to decide programs and policies for themselves, to manage their own affairs, to govern themselves, and to control their land and its resources. It insists on the inviolability of their land and on the strict observance and protection of obligations and rights guaranteed the Indians by treaties with the federal government.

There is nothing startling about any of this. For generations — until historic new federal attitudes emerged in 1970 — the Indians were governed, like colonial subjects, by the Bureau of Indian Affairs of the Department of the Interior. An untrusting, sometimes corrupt, and often incompetent white man's bureaucracy, accountable in practice to Congress and the Bureau of the Budget rather than to the Indians, it exercised autocratic veto powers over all aspects of Indian life that were important to the Indians and perpetuated and spread abroad the myth that Indians were not intelligent or competent enough to manage their own affairs.

To the bureau, as to the patronizing do-gooders, Red Power advocacy was an unsettling force. It asserted angrily that Indian peoples were, and always had been, intelligent, competent humans. Their history before the coming of the whites demonstrated that they managed their own affairs as well as, if not better than, white men were now managing the affairs of the modern, non-Indian world. Indian societies, it stated, were usually just right for the conditions and environments of the individual peoples, who protected the environment and lived in harmony with nature and the cosmos. There was no reason to believe that the Indians on their own could not once again create—better and faster than any white man could make for them—societies that harmonized with the environments in which they existed, the resources they possessed, and the limitations of the surrounding white societies. If there was a successful future that could be envisioned for Indian peoples who achieved the right of self-determination, it was of tribal groups on their own federally protected lands, which were made economically viable by Indian-determined programs. The programs—assisted, where requested, by the expertise of technicians and specialists and by adequate funding and credit—would be organized and managed by the Indians, just as non-Indians ran their own townships, counties, or other community units. The tribal lands, in this view, would be administered by and for Indians, with Indians controlling their own local governments, courts, funds, schools, and other public institutions.

Beginning in the late 1960's, the federal government began evidencing awareness of the Indians' growing pressure for the right of self-determination, and in 1970 President Nixon, acknowledging that the Indians should have that right, called on Congress to join him in bringing about its realization. At the same time, the Bureau of Indian Affairs, putting more

Indians into top, policy-making positions, initiated long-needed structural and philosophical changes designed to make itself more responsive to the needs of the Indian people and give the tribes full opportunities to control their own affairs.

Much still remained to be done, however, in the way of implementing the new intentions, and by the end of 1970 the Indians' fight for freedom had already entered a new and more militant phase. Where Red Power advocacy had previously taken the form of demands, petitions, meetings, and with a few exceptions, demonstrations that were peaceful, a growing desperation and sense that official ears were closed and minds locked induced small but increasingly numerous groups of Indians in all parts of the country to take action on their own behalf. Alcatraz had been occupied late in 1969 as a symbol of the Indians' new determination to go on the offensive for their rights. Other organized confrontations, some successful and some not, occurred in rapid succession in New York, Michigan, South Dakota, California, Washington State, Wisconsin, Colorado, Massachusetts, and elsewhere. Although the motives differed (some were to retake land that the Indians had never ceded, some were to oust white interlopers on Indian lands, and some were to defend treaty rights), all the actions reflected a growing awareness among Indians that Red Power could be more than a slogan.

The aim of Red, or Indian, Power — the right of Indians to be free of colonialist rule and to run their own affairs, with security for their lands and rights — is the major theme of contemporary Indian affairs and of this book. The theme has many facets: the continuing struggle by the Indians for protection of their lands and treaty rights, including promised services; for water and hunting and fishing rights; for the kind of educational system they want for their children; for the lifting of the colonialists' heavy hands from their daily affairs; for protection of Indians who go to the white man's cities; for acknowledgment of their right to be Indians; and for many other things that inhibit and hobble their struggle not merely to solve their problems their way, but quite often to survive. All this is part of the mass of injustices and oppression that lie hidden below the water — the base of the enduring social and economic problems.

Not all the many facets of Indian concerns of today are treated in detail in the writings and documents that make up this book. To do justice to the many aspects of modern-day Indian affairs would require a series of volumes. But in sum the materials that follow, arranged in general in chronological sequence, should make clear the scope and nature of the Indians' present fight for self-determination, self-government, and the right to make their own decisions and manage their own affairs. As significant materials in the recent history of Indian affairs, they illuminate the road along which a new generation of patriot Indians have been moving in their fight to be free from the white man's paternalism and to survive as tribal peoples in modern-day American society.

THE INDIAN RESERVATION SYSTEM

by Thomas L. Sloan

Although it has always exercised sovereignty over the territory lying within its borders, the United States acknowledged from the beginning that the various Indian tribes owned the land. From time to time, as the whites spread westward, the government bought or took land from the Indians and opened it to white settlement. What the government did not buy, or otherwise take, it reserved for the Indians, and they were forced to move onto these remaining parts of their lands and stay out of the way of the whites.

In actual practice, the acquisition of the Indians' land was a long, sordid story, for often the land was overrun by whites before the government had had a chance to buy it, and many times the Indians lost their land by fraud, theft, or war. But in one way or another, the government either left some land for the tribes or set aside special land for them, promising to protect those reservations and provide various services to the Indians on them.

These promises were made as payment for the lands that the Indians had sold or lost to the people of the United States. Usually they were made part of the treaty in which the Indians gave up title to their land. Covering various Indian rights and government obligations, they are regarded by the Indians as their treaty rights, representing the sacred word of the federal government.

Simultaneously, through numerous statutes and laws, the government took over the management of the Indians' affairs on their reservations. That, too, was a sordid story marked by graft, corruption, neglect, and the tyranny of missionaries, army officers, and petty despots of the Department of the Interior over the lives of the dispossessed and defeated native peoples.

Until recently the remoteness of reservation life from the mainstream of American affairs kept the Indians out of sight and out of mind of the average non-Indian American. But through the years, as paternalism and oppression reigned on the reservations, an occasional Indian voice was raised against the tormentors.

In 1911 a group of six Indian intellectuals, who had created places for themselves in the white man's world, founded the Society of American Indians. After enlarging their membership, they held a national conference in Columbus, Ohio, in October of that year. The society's purpose was to promote the interests of the Indians of the United States, and at the conference a number of talented Indians delivered papers on various Indian problems.

One of the papers, criticizing government injustices on the reservations, was read by Thomas L. Sloan, an Omaha Indian. Sloan, who was one of the founders of the society, later edited the group's journal, *The American Indian Magazine,* and became president of the organization, which seems to have come to an end about 1930.

In its winter issue of 1970, *The Indian Historian,* published by the American Indian Historical Society in San Francisco, reprinted Sloan's 1911 address, which is excerpted below. In commenting on the content of the speech, as well as on other papers delivered by the Indian speakers at the conference of that pioneer Indian organization, *The Indian Historian* noted, "They speak of 'problems,' and deal with them in a most practical way. What is so extraordinary and exasperating, is that these very problems still exist today, but in a much more aggravated form."

Since the advent of civilized government on this continent, the Indian has been recognized as the subject of the dominant power claiming and holding the territory. While treaties were made with all the solemnity of international law, still the Indian tribes were within the power and jurisdiction of the dominant government. They were not separate nations within the judgment of civilized governments who among themselves made treaties which they respected. The civilized nations made treaties with the Indians as a matter of expediency.

Early in the administration of Indian affairs it became evident that the Indian could not rely upon the statements of the Indian Service officials, the laws made by Congress for their protection, nor the treaties made between them and the United States of America. The rights to hunt, to fish, to make homes and to occupy the lands of their fathers were never held sacred to the Indian, although declared to be so by law or treaty. Public policy and political policy joined in the administration to deprive him of his rights.

In Arizona, New Mexico and Colorado an official first named to protect his water interests, without which the lands were of no value, recommended that he hold his rights under the State and territorial laws. This was in States where the Indian's rights are least considered, and where it is the practice to steal water and take advantage by the use of it. This protecting Indian official wanted those rights turned over to the State. He even admits under oath that where the courts have decreed that a certain quantity of water on specifically described lands, he, as an official of the Indian Office, ignored the decrees of the court, the previously acquired water rights and the established rule of law as announced by the court for the protection of Indian lands and water. When asked what he had done to recover the stolen water rights for the Indians, he said he did not think it right to take it away from the whites who had used it so long. He was paid to protect and look after the interests of the Indian, but he had no desire to recover that which belonged to him. The long years of use by the Indian had no effect upon him as to their established water rights. But when it had been stolen from them by the whites and used for a shorter time, it was wrong to take it from them and give it back to the Indians to whom it belonged. That is an example of administration protection, and a disgrace to the nation, against which complaint should be made. . . .

. . . The idea of the Indian Office seems to be that they are better fitted to handle all the affairs of the Indian than the Indian himself, or the other departments of a republican form of government. The Indian Office says, "The Indian does not know what is best for him in the administration of these inheritances." So a politician is selected to act as judge for them, and this politician acting as judge violates every rule of law for the protection of property, and the Indian [is] subjected to rules and regulations and arbitrary action that violates constitutional limitations. The evil seems to be that the Indian Bureau administers as if the Indian was selected for their benefit, to exploit them, and not they that were created for the benefit of the Indian. This spirit prevails generally in the Indian service.

It seems that there is no step forward in the Indian service. With less lands now to administer, with fewer ignorant Indians, they still have more employees, greater expenditures, and a greater per capita cost to maintain their work than before. More rules and regulations, and when an Indian learns to comply with one set of rules and regulations they are changed so that he is compelled to begin again.

Although the President of the United States appointed a so-called competency commission to determine the competency of the Omaha Indians, and they made their report, which was approved, and the Indians declared competent, still the superintendent in charge may, without hearing or notice of any kind, declare a citizen Indian of the tribe to be incompetent. Should the superintendent in charge report favorably upon any such man, a clerk or some one else in the Indian Office may overrule it, and the communications which are submitted to the Indian Office are treated as confidential and therefore not open to an investigation by the party affected. It is in effect a star chamber proceeding that determines that a citizen of the United States is an incompetent person. Their status as men and women determined in such a manner is not by law, but by autocratic and arbitrary power. The practice of subjecting a man or woman to investigation without notice, hearing or trial, and declaring him or her incompetent upon a secret order, is one that cannot be defended under any circumstances. Such men and women, being citizens of the United States and of the States wherein they live, are entitled to all the rights, privileges and immunities of citizens of the several States, but they are treated as arbitrarily as the subjects of the Czar of Russia. Men, through political accident, and most likely through business failure preceding it, are placed in positions of arbitrary power. They evolve new theories, discover latent powers, old and new wrongs, and remedies for all. They are followed by a horde of their appointees who know nothing more than themselves about the people and their conditions. About the time they have discovered their success or failure some new politician is found or some "land duck" requires a berth. Then begins some new idea.

The local communities about the reservation always desire

something to be done with it. The representatives of the business people of the town adjoining a reservation desire that the land be obtained in fee, sold or otherwise disposed of, not for the welfare of the Indian, but to enable them to develop business or trade. Business men, politicians, farmers, railroad men, grafters and sharks in the vicinity of a reservation wish it open, not for the benefit of the Indian, but for a larger opportunity for each in his own line. Such influences reach the executive branches of the government as well as Congress more readily than the Indian, and when something is to be done with the Indian land or property under the general guise of some good for him, he is the last person to know about it, through some action taken that affects his property or his income. . . .

Sales of Indian land have been made under the directions of agency officials. Usually the Indians, before the sale, obtained more money in a year from rentals than they can get from the proceeds of the sale of the land in the same length of time while held in the agency office. In some cases after the sale of such lands and its dissipations in a few years, the Indian is without any income at all, and he would have had an income through rents during that same period, an amount equal to the sum which was paid to him from the principal. The money is held at the agency for the sale of land, which furnishes some means of living, and the only means of living for many Indians.

On the Rosebud Reservation it costs the Indian as much in time and money and effort to collect the small sums of money at the agency as it would to have gone out and earned it. Others with sums of money at the agency have suffered in want. One old man past seventy years of age, living near Bonesteel, on what was formerly a part of the Rosebud Sioux Reservation, was told in a letter from the Office at Washington, in answer to his application to be paid some money, that if he would go to the agency he would receive from his four thousand dollars there on deposit such amount of money as would be necessary to provide for his needs. It was one hundred and fifty miles across the country to the agency. To go around by railroad was more than three hundred miles, and the stage route twenty-five miles more. He had neither the means nor the physical ability to make the trip, and this particular old man died in absolute want, except such means as were provided him by the neighbors. An inspector of the Indian service says there are many such cases.

An old Indian woman past eighty years of age, in order to get from the agency a check of ten dollars, money due her derived from the sale of her land, had to travel seven or eight miles each month to get the check. During the severest kind of cold weather, about the 1st of January, it was necessary for her grandson to carry her to the wagon and cover her carefully and drive a distance of seven or eight miles and return, and the hardship upon that old lady was more than it was worth to get it. Had she paid her grandson a reasonable compensation for taking care of her there, she should have had five or six dollars left out of the ten dollars that was paid her.

The ration system is no worse than the present money system, which holds the Indian a bondsman and makes him eke out the same kind of living or existence that he had when he received the rations. It takes from him every incentive for development, and holds him in such subjection that his independence and manliness are destroyed. He gets no experience, and he is subservient at all times through the control of this money to the agency official and to the reservation system. . . .

No man in Washington, neither the head nor the subordinate, can know the conditions of the man or his opportunities or his capabilities. The Indians are individuals and are not bound directly or controlled by any set of rules and regulations which may be promulgated by the Secretary of the Interior or the Commissioner of Indian Affairs. The man on the ground, the agency official, is overwhelmed by official duties and does not know, perhaps does not care, about the individual; he has more than he can do, and he is expected to do that which only the individual can do for himself. He is not given a chance to get away from supervision long enough to assert his individuality, and it may be that he will only develop manliness after he has been defrauded out of his lands or has frittered it away. At any rate the present system is not making men and women. There is a lack of development of the man in dealing with the Indians. . . .

. . . In the administration of Indian affairs there should be such reforms as will give the Indian in hearings and investigations those rights which belong to him under the Constitution of the United States. That his property may be protected by regular court proceedings, and that when the court decrees certain rights, no Indian official be permitted to disregard the decree of the court and the law protecting the Indian, and not to violate his own oath of office to the detriment of the Indian. . . . We are having these lands administered in a manner that is a shame and a disgrace to any civilized nation, let alone these United States, and we ought to ask for such reform as will guarantee to us the protection of the laws and the privileges with reference to our property rights, which are given to every citizen, and for that matter, to non-citizens who hold property within the United States.

INDIAN SELF-GOVERNMENT

by Felix S. Cohen

Acknowledgment of the Indians' right of self-government is not new. In fact, since the early days of the republic many men in and out of government have urged that the Indians be allowed to govern themselves. Laws have been passed with the premise that the government would eventually step aside and let the Indians run their own affairs, and even when other laws conferred on the Department of the Interior certain powers over the Indians, they frequently stipulated that the powers were temporary and that they should be transferred to the Indians as soon as possible.

But such designs were never realized, and the government's strangle hold over the Indians' affairs grew progressively tighter. Some of this history is related in the following article written by Felix S. Cohen, a distinguished legal philosopher, battler for Indian rights, and the author of the *Handbook of Federal Indian Law*. From 1933 to 1948 Cohen was assistant solicitor of the Department of the Interior, where he rendered notable service in behalf of the Indians. After leaving the government, he entered private law practice and taught at City College in New York and at the Yale Law School. But as general counsel of the Association on American Indian Affairs, he continued, both as a lawyer and as an author, to champion Indian causes until his death in 1953 at the age of forty-six.

Many of his writings on Indian affairs are still relevant in the 1970's. This one, a persuasive commentary on the nature of self-government and its applicability to the federal government's relations with Indians, was published in *The American Indian* in 1949.

Not all who speak of self-government mean the same thing by the term. Therefore let me say at the outset that by self-government I mean that form of government in which decisions are made not by the people who are wisest, or ablest, or closest to some throne in Washington or in Heaven, but, rather by the people who are most directly affected by the decisions. I think that if we conceive of self-government in these matter-of-fact terms, we may avoid some confusion.

Let us admit that self-government includes graft, corruption, and the making of decisions by inexpert minds. Certainly these are features of self-government in white cities and counties, and so we ought not to be scared out of our wits if somebody jumps up in the middle of a discussion of Indian self-government and shouts "graft" or "corruption."

Self-government is not a new or radical idea. Rather, it is one of the oldest staple ingredients of the American way of life. Many Indians in this country enjoyed self-government long before European immigrants who came to these shores did. It took the white colonists north of the Rio Grande about 170 years to rid themselves of the traditional European pattern of the divine right of kings or, what we call today, the long arm of bureaucracy, and to substitute the less efficient but more satisfying Indian pattern of self-government. South of the Rio Grande the process took more than three centuries, and there are some who are still skeptical as to the completeness of the shift.

This is not the time and place to discuss the ways in which the Indian pattern of self-government undermined the patterns which the colonists first brought to this country, patterns of feudalism, landlordism and serfdom, economic monopoly and special privilege, patterns of religious intolerance and nationalism and the divine right of kings. It was not only Franklin and Jefferson who went to school with Indian teachers, like the Iroquois statesman Canasatego, to learn the ways of federal union and democracy. It was no less the great political thinkers of Europe, in the years following the discovery of the New World, who undermined ancient dogmas when they saw spread before them on the panorama of the Western Hemisphere new societies in which liberty, equality, and fraternity were more perfectly realized than they were realized in contemporary Europe, societies in which government drew its just powers from the consent of the governed. To Vitoria, Grotius, Locke, Montaigne, Montesquieu, Voltaire, and Rousseau, Indian liberty and self-government provided a new polestar in political thinking. But, for the present, I want merely to emphasize that Indian self-government is not a new or radical policy but an ancient fact. It is not something friends of the Indians can confer upon the Indians. Nobody can grant self-government to anybody else. We all recall that when Alexander was ruler of most of the known civilized world, he once visited the philosopher Diogenes, who was making his home in an old bathtub. Diogenes was a rich man because he did not want anything that he did not have. He was a mighty man because he could master himself. Alexander admired Diogenes for these qualities, and standing before him said, "Oh, Diogenes, if there is anything that I can grant you, tell me and I will grant it." To which Diogenes replied, "You are standing in my sunlight. Get out of the way." The Federal Government which is, to-day, the dominant power of the civilized world cannot give self-government to an Indian community. All it can really do for self-government is to get out of the way.

In the history of Western thought, theologians, missionaries, judges, and legislators for 400 years and more have consistently recognized the right of Indians to manage their own affairs. Nothing that we could say today in defense of Indian rights of self-government could be as eloquent as the words of Francisco de Vitoria in 1532 or of Pope Paul III in 1537 or of Bartholomew de las Casas in 1542 or of Chief Justice Marshall in 1832. For 400 years, men who have looked at the matter without the distortions of material prejudice or bureaucratic power have seen that the safety and freedom of all of us is inevitably tied up with the safety and freedom of the weakest and the tiniest of our minorities. This is not novel vision but ancient wisdom.

What gives point to the problem in 1949 is that after 422 years of support for the principle of Indian self-government, in the thinking of the western world, there is so little Indian self-government. Here we have, I think, the main problem on which I should like to throw the light of a few concrete examples and incidents.

I recall very vividly in 1934 working on a study for the Indian Office of legal rights of Indian tribes which was to serve as a guide in the drafting of tribal constitutions under the Wheeler-Howard Act. I found that the laws and court decisions clearly recognized that Indian tribes have all the governmental rights of any state or municipality except in so far as those rights have been curtailed or qualified by Act of Congress or by treaty, and such qualifications are relatively minor, in fact. When, at last, my job was done and the Solicitor's opinion had been reviewed and approved by the proper authorities of the Interior Department and properly mimeographed, I learned to my dismay that all copies of the opinion in the Indian Office had been carefully hidden away in a cabinet and that when an Indian was found reading this opinion, the copy was forthwith taken from his hands and placed under lock and key. Incidentally, the Indian whose reading was thus interrupted had spent more years in school and college than the men who controlled the lock and key. The Indian Office was sure that the opinion, if released to the public, would be most disturbing. I suppose they were right. The opinion was disturbing to the Indian Office. Its suppression was equally disturbing to me. My despondency was somewhat relieved when I found that Chief Justice Marshall and Pope Paul III and Bartholomew de las Casas had all received the same treatment. It was of John Marshall's decision upholding the rights of self-government of the Cherokee Tribe that an old Indian fighter in the White House, President Jackson, said, "John Marshall has made his decision. Now let him enforce it." The sovereign State of Georgia paid no attention to the decision of the United States Supreme Court and the good missionary whom the Supreme Court had freed continued to languish in a Georgia prison. And what happened to John Marshall in 1832 was not novel. The same thing happened to Bartholomew de las Casas 300 years earlier when, as Archbishop of Chiapas, he endeavored to read to his flock of Spanish landowners the guarantees of Indian freedom signed by the Pope and by the King of Spain. He was not allowed to read these documents by the outraged landowners of his archdiocese. In fact, he was driven from his church. History has a strange way of repeating itself. I was relieved to find myself in such good company, and so, instead of resigning, I distributed copies of the opinion where I thought they would do the most good.

How can we explain the fact that despite all the respect and reverence shown to the principle of Indian self-government across four centuries, there is so little left today of the fact of Indian self-government? How can we explain this discrepancy between word and deed?

The simplest explanation, of course, and the one that is easiest for simple, unsophisticated Indians to understand is the explanation in terms of white man's hypocrisy.

I think we must go deeper into the wellsprings of human conduct and belief to understand what is happening in the field of Indian self-government and to relate facts to words.

Double-talk is not always a sign of hypocrisy. Probably the easiest way of maintaining consistency in our principles is to have a second-string substitute vocabulary to use in describing any facts that do not fit into the vocabulary of our professed principles. Thus, if we believe in liberty and find that some particular exercise of liberty is annoying, we may call that license, rather than liberty. So it is possible to talk about the virtues and values of self-government without allowing this talk to influence our conduct in any way, if we have a substitute vocabulary handy which will permit us to dismiss the appeal for self-government in any concrete case, without using the term "self-government." The second vocabulary to which professed believers in self-government continually turn when concrete cases arise is the vocabulary that talks about "a state within a state," "segregation," and, in the words of the Hoover Report, "progressive measures to integrate the Indians into the rest of the population as the best solution of 'the Indian problem.'"

There are two answers to this double-talk: One is to deny the clichés and to insist that there is nothing wrong about having a state within a state; that, in fact, this is the whole substance of American federalism and tolerance. We may go on to say that the right of people to segregate themselves and to mix with their own kind and their own friends, is a part of the right, of privacy and liberty, and that the enjoyment of this right, the right to be different, is one of the most valuable parts of the American way of life. We may say further that it is not the business of the Indian Bureau or of any other federal agency to integrate Indians or Jews or Catholics or Negroes or Holy Rollers or Jehovah's Witnesses into the rest of the population as a solution of the Indian, Jewish, Negro, or Catholic problem, or any other problem; but that it is the duty of the federal government to respect the right of any group to be different so long as it does not violate the criminal law.

Apart from this challenging of clichés, there is a second cure for the habit of double-talk in our discussions of Indian self-government. That remedy is to reject what Stuart Chase called "the tyranny of words" and to think facts.

The great American philosopher, Ralph Barton Perry, coined the phrase, "the egocentric predicament" to call attention to the fact that each of us is at the center of his world and cannot help seeing the world through his own eyes and from his own position. It takes a certain amount of sophistication to realize that the vision of others who see the world from different perspectives is just as valid as our own. One of the striking features of the administrative or bureaucratic mind is that it lacks such sophistication. Thus, it often turns out that the officials who have most to say in praise of Indian self-government have a certain blind spot where Indian self-government comes close to their own activities.

I recall that when we were helping Indians draft the constitutions and charters which were supposed to be the vehicles of self-government under the Wheeler-Howard Act, all of the Indian Bureau officials were very strongly in favor of self-government, and in favor of allowing all tribes to exercise to the full extent their inherent legal rights. There was only one difficulty. The people of the Education Division were in favor of self-government in forestry, credit, leasing, law and order, and every other field of social activity except education. Of course, education, they thought, was a highly technical matter in which tribal council politics should have no part. Education should be left to the experts, according to the experts, and the experts were to be found in the Education Division. Similarly, with the Forestry Division. They were all in favor of self-government with respect to education, credit, agricultural leases, law and order, and everything else except for forestry. Forestry, of course, involved matters of particular complexity and difficulty in which the experts ought to make the decisions, and the experts, of course, were to be found in the Forestry Division. So it was with the Credit Section, the Leasing Section, the Law and Order Division, and all the other divisions and subdivisions of the Indian Bureau. The result was that while every official was in favor of self-government generally, by the same token he was opposed to self-government in the particular field over which he had any jurisdiction. In that field he could see very clearly the advantages of the expert knowledge which he and his staff had accumulated, and the disadvantages of lay judgment influenced by so-called political considerations which would be involved in decisions of local councils.

Those of us in the Department who had been given a special responsibility for protecting Indian tribal self-government finally went to the Commissioner and pointed out that if we followed the traditional practice of yielding to each expert division on the matter with which it was concerned, there would be no Indian self-government. There was a long and bloody argument and eventually the Commissioner upheld the principle which is now written into most Indian tribal charters, that the Indians themselves, at some point or other, may dispense with supervisory controls over most of their various activities. Some of the charters include a special probationary period of five years or ten years, during which leases and contracts are subject to Departmental control. In many cases, particularly among the Oklahoma tribes, this period has terminated and the Indians are free, if they choose to do so, to make their own leases and contracts and various other economic decisions without Departmental control. That, at least, is what the charters and constitutions say.

Yet I must add that instances have been called to my attention where decisions and ordinances that were not supposed to be subject to review by superintendents or by the Commissioner of Indian Affairs have been rescinded or vetoed by these officials. Tribes without independent legal guidance frequently acquiesce in such infringements upon their constitutional and corporate powers. Thus many of the gains of the Roosevelt era are being chipped away.

Let me give one more instance of the egocentric predicament in action. A certain Southwestern superintendent recently wrote an eloquent article in defense of Indian self-government, and in support of the idea that the Indian Bureau should work itself out of its job. A few weeks later some of the tribes under his jurisdiction decided that they needed legal assistance and proceeded to employ attorneys to help them handle their own leasing, grazing and social security problems. At this point all sorts of reasons began to occur to the superintendent why the tribes under his agency should not be allowed to select their own attorneys. In fact, for many months, as fast as one of his objections was met another objection occurred to him.

Here is a superintendent who is doing the best thing, as he sees it, for his Indians. He is, I believe, entirely sincere. Recently he explained that if one of these attorney contracts were approved he would be out of a job, so far as this particular tribe was concerned. Now you will recall that this is the same superintendent who wrote an article urging that the Indian Bureau work itself out of a job. But when the matter came to an issue in concrete terms affecting his own job, he saw the question in a different light. That is only human. That is a part of the egocentric predicament. And it is that predicament which makes the adherents and defenders of self-government so much more dangerous to the cause of Indian self-government than any outright adversaries. If self-government were a man it might repeat, "God preserve me from my friends. I can take care of my enemies."

Unfortunately, it is not the tribal decisions which we agree with that test our belief in the right of self-government. It is decisions that we loathe and believe to be fraught with death that test our beliefs in tribal self-government, just as it is religious opinions that we loathe and believe to be fraught with death that test our belief in religious tolerance. But it takes a vast amount of sophistication or philosophy to say what Justice Holmes once said, "I think we should be eternally vigilant against attempts to check the expression of opinion that we loathe and believe to be fraught with death." Allowing others to express opinions we agree with is no test at all of our belief in free speech. To quote again from Justice Holmes: "But when men have realized that time has upset many fighting faiths, they may come to believe even more than they believe in the very foundations of their own conduct, that the ultimate good desired is better reached by free trade in ideas."

May we not profit, may not the world profit, if in a few places in our Western Hemisphere there is still freedom of an aboriginal people to try out ideas of self-government, of economics, of social relations, that we consider to be wrong? After all, there are so many places all over the world where we Americans can try out the ideas of economics and government that we know to be right. Is there not a great scientific advantage in allowing alternative ideas to work themselves out to a point where they can demonstrate the evils that we believe are bound to flow from a municipal government that maintains no prisons, or from a government that gives land to all members of the group who need it? Are we not lucky that the areas within which these governmental ideas can work from themselves out are so small that they cannot possibly corrupt the nation or the world?

Indeed, is there not a possibility that we can learn from example—horrible examples, perhaps, or perhaps examples to be emulated? Have we not been learning from Indian examples for a good many years? Have we not been taking over all sorts of horrifying Indian customs, disrespect for kings and other duly appointed authorities, the smoking of poisonous weeds, like tobacco, and the eating of poisonous plant products, like tomatoes, potatoes, tapioca, and quinine, not to mention cocoa and cocaine? Of course, we must all of us start with the assumption that we are right or as near being right as we can be. But can we not also recognize, with Justice Holmes, that time has upset many fighting faiths, and that even if we are possessed of absolute truth it is worthwhile to have somebody somewhere trying out a different idea?

Just as serious as the habit of double-talk or the egocentric predicament is the method of procrastination as a way of avoiding the concrete implications of Indian self-government. On May 20, 1834, not 1934 but 1834, the House Committee on Indian Affairs reported that a large part of the activity of the Indian Bureau was being carried on in violation of law and without any statutory authority. It urged that the Indian Bureau work itself out of a job by turning over the various jobs in the Bureau itself to the Indians and by placing the Indian Bureau employees on the various reservations under the control of the various Indian tribes. These recommendations were written into law. They are still law. The justice of these recommendations has not been challenged for 115 years. But always the answer of the Indian Bureau is: Give us more time. We must wait until more Indians have gone to college, until the Indians are rich, until the Indians are skilled in politics and able to overlook traditional jealousies, until the Indians are experts in all the fields in which the Indian Bureau now employs experts. But we are never told how the Indians are to achieve these goals without participation in their own government. And so perhaps some of us are entitled to look with a skeptical eye upon the new legislative proposals by which the Indian Bureau is to work itself out of a job after the usual interim 10 year or 20 year period of increased appropriations.

What provokes skepticism is the fact that the various bills which are being introduced into Congress to achieve this objective generally end up by giving new powers and new millions of dollars not to the Indian tribal councils but to the Indian Bureau. And when we find that specific dates are not attached to any promised transfers of power to the tribes, we are entitled to be skeptical. The record shows that for more than one hundred years the aggrandizement of Indian Bureau power has been justified on the ground that this was merely needed for a brief temporary period until authority could be conveyed over to the Indians themselves.

Indian Bureau government, like other forms of colonialism, starts from the basic premise that government is a matter of knowledge or wisdom. If we accept this basic premise, there is no answer to the aristocratic argument of Alexander Hamilton that government should be handled by the rich, the well born, and the able. If it be said that rich people and well born people are not necessarily able, the obvious answer is that those who are rich or well born are at least more likely to have expert knowledge, training, and experience than those who are poor or the children of poor families, and that in government we must proceed by general rules, under which it is safe to say that the rich, the well born, and the able will do a more expert job than others in the posts of government. One of the greatest of our Secretaries of the Interior, also, like Hamilton, an immigrant from lands that worshipped empire, Carl Schurz, once said to an Indian group that was inclined to object to the activities of some local agency personnel: "The Great Father is a very wise man. He knows everything. If there is anything wrong with your agent, he will know it before either you or I know it."

I think that if government were merely a matter of wisdom and expert knowledge, the argument of Carl Schurz and Alexander Hamilton would be irrefutable. The answer to Schurz and to Hamilton is that government is not a science; it is not primarily a matter of wisdom or technique or efficiency. Government is a matter chiefly of human purpose and of justice, which depends upon human purpose. And each of us is a more faithful champion of his own purposes than any expert. The basic principle of American liberty is distrust of expert rulers, and recognition, in Acton's words, that power corrupts and that absolute power corrupts absolutely. That is why America, despite all the lingo of the administrative experts, has insisted upon self-government rather than "good government," and has insisted that experts should be servants, not masters. And what we insist upon in the governing of these United States, our Indian fellow-citizens also like to enjoy in their limited domains; the right to use experts when their advice is wanted and the right to reject their advice when it conflicts with purposes on which we are all our own experts. The classical answer to the Hamilton-Schurz-Indian Bureau philosophy of "expert government" is the answer given by Thomas Jefferson in a letter to the Cherokee Indians in 1808. Jefferson said: "The fool has as great a right to express his opinion by vote as the wise, because he is equally free and equally master of himself."

Recently I heard repeated the words of Nazi Admiral Doenitz, as he faced his judges at the conclusion of the Nuremberg Trial. The principle of expert leadership, he said, had proved itself in the armed forces as a principle of efficiency. It seemed to him that the same principle would prove itself in the field of government, but the results showed that the leadership principle in government had brought in its train only ghastly destruction.

Let us hope that we will not have to wait and see, as Admiral Doenitz saw, what happens when self-government and minority rights are subordinated to expert government and the leadership principle. Let us be thankful that in this country we have, in laboratory proportions before us, in proportions so small that the individual effort of half a dozen of us can make a real difference, this perennial conflict between democratic self-government and the various modern forms of aristocracy, or government by experts. The issue we face is not the issue merely of whether Indians will regain their independence of spirit. Our interest in Indian self-government today is not the interest of sentimentalists or antiquarians. We have a vital concern with Indian self-government because the Indian is to America what the Jew was to the Russian Czars and Hitler's Germany. For us, the Indian tribe is the miners' canary and when it flutters and droops we know that the poison gasses of intolerance threaten all other minorities in our land. And who of us is not a member of some minority?

The issue is not only an issue of Indian rights; it is the much larger one of whether American liberty can be preserved. If we fight only for our *own* liberty because it is our own, are we any better than the dog who fights for his bone? We must believe in liberty itself to defend it effectively. What is my own divides me from my fellow man. Liberty, which is the other side of the shield of tolerance, is a social affair that unites me with my fellow man. If we fight for civil liberties for our side, we show that we believe not in civil liberties but in our side. But when those of us who never were Indians and never expect to be Indians fight for the cause of Indian self-government, we are fighting for something that is not limited by the accidents of race and creed and birth; we are fighting for what Las Casas and Vitoria and Pope Paul III called the integrity or salvation of our own souls. We are fighting for what Jefferson called the basic rights of man. We are fighting for the last best hope of earth. And these are causes that should carry us through many defeats.

A PROGRAM FOR INDIAN CITIZENS

A Summary Report of the Commission
on the Rights, Liberties, and
Responsibilities of the American Indian
January, 1961

The Bureau of Indian Affairs, the condition of the Indians, and the status of federal-Indian relations have been the subjects of many public and private studies, congressional investigations, and governmental task force reports. Perhaps the most significant study ever made is the Meriam Report, a survey directed by Lewis Meriam under the auspices of the Institute for Government Research and issued in 1928 under the title "The Problems of Indian Administration." Its findings about the condition of the tribes shocked the nation and led to the passage of the Wheeler-Howard Act, better known as the Indian Reorganization Act, in 1934.

The principal effect of that New Deal act was to halt a reservation-impoverishing allotment policy that stemmed from the Dawes General Allotment Act of 1887, whose intent had been to hasten the Indians' assimilation by breaking up the reservations into individual allotments for each Indian family. Tribal ties and organizations were to disappear, and the Indians were to become individual farmers and homeowners like the whites. For many reasons the allotment policy was a failure. In fact, its net result—foreseen by many of the opponents of the Dawes Act—was to deepen the Indians' poverty and helplessness by selling off to whites Indian reservation land that was left over after allotments had been made to the Indians. This loss of valuable resources (90 million acres out of a total of 138 million acres that the Indians had owned in 1887) was attacked by the Meriam Report and stopped by the Indian Reorganization Act.

The legislation of 1934 included, in addition, many reforms that were intended to halt the injustices on the reservations and point the Indians on a road to progress. It encouraged the creation of tribal councils and constitutions, though the Department of the Interior, despite the efforts of persons like Felix

Cohen, allowed the councils to be little more than figureheads and continued to thwart self-government by retaining for itself veto power and ultimate authority over most reservation affairs, including financial and legal matters. The act extended a minimum of financial credit to the tribes and restored certain freedoms to the Indians (in an ironic gesture, these first Americans had been granted citizenship by their conquerors in 1924, but many personal freedoms and civil rights, including the practice of their religious beliefs, had been—and in some cases still are—curtailed). It commenced an improvement in the Indians' economies and educational and health facilities, and it promoted a revival of Indian cultures.

The act was administered under a sympathetic Indian commissioner, John Collier, and the atmosphere began to change for the better on many reservations. But the failure of the government to give the Indians the right and responsibility to run their own affairs, together with inadequate funding for the act by Congress and the continued hamstringing by Interior's bureaucracy, doomed the new policy. Indian assimilation, still the intent of Congress, seemed to be proceeding no faster than it had under the Dawes Act, and in 1953 the passage of House Concurrent Resolution 108 by the Eighty-third Congress—an impatient attempt to speed the assimilation process and end federal expenditures for Indians by declaring Congress' new intention to terminate federal relations with the tribes at the earliest possible date and let the Indians "progress" like all other Americans—brought to a sharp halt whatever progress had been made under the Reorganization Act.

The new "termination" policy was a disaster. Several tribes, including the Menominees in Wisconsin and the Klamaths in Oregon, were hastily and ill-advisedly "terminated" and plunged close to economic and social chaos. Policies and programs within the Bureau of Indian Affairs were halted, reversed, or redesigned to hasten the tribes to termination. Indian cultures and pride in Indianness were again frowned on. All tribes felt the renewed threat of loss of lands and forced assimilation and became immobilized; ready or not, they faced the dread prospect of being handed over to the states, most if not all of which could not or would not assume the protective responsibilities, services, and other obligations that the federal government had originally assumed by treaties and various agreements in the past and that the tribes still urgently required.

The application of the termination policy, which almost immediately brought hardships, new problems, and results exactly opposite to what had been intended, aroused increasing protests from the tribes, persons knowledgeable about Indian affairs, state legislators, governors, and congressmen, who criticized the policy as premature, ill-advised, and wrong because it was imposed on tribes without their consent. The inadvisability of proceeding with implementation of the policy finally became clear to Congress and the Eisenhower administration, and on September 18, 1958, Secretary of the Interior

Fred A. Seaton announced that no tribe thereafter would be terminated without its consent and that the thrust of federal Indian policy would be redirected toward the health, education, and economic development of the Indians.

By then, however, serious and enduring damage had been done to the progress of the Indians and to federal-Indian relations. The Indians were suspicious of the government and either hostile or passively resistant to policies and programs. The programs themselves were confused and largely undermined, for a fuzziness existed about just what the national Indian policy was. A Summary Report on Indian Affairs by the Commission on the Rights, Liberties, and Responsibilities of the American Indian, released by the Fund for the Republic, Inc., in January, 1961, stated: "From the date of Seaton's speech until 1961, confusion has existed, the Secretary seeming to espouse one policy and the Bureau of Indian Affairs another. All the time, moreover, Joint Resolution 108, stating the policy of Congress, has been in effect." This report of the Commission on the Rights, Liberties, and Responsibilities of the American Indian, issued under the title "A Program for Indian Citizens," concerned government attitudes toward the Indians and the translation of those attitudes into methods for the implementation of programs. It recognized Congress' desire to achieve assimilation as quickly as possible, and it did not argue with that goal. But, somewhat gingerly, it implied that the methods had been all wrong: instead of stamping out Indian culture and values (that is, stripping the Indianness off Indians so they would have no alternative save to become whites, a policy much like that of killing all the buffalo so the Indians would have to go on reservations under the authority of ration-giving agents or starve), the commission argued, the government could speed the Indians' progress by permitting them to retain pride in their Indianness and thenceforth fashioning federal programs more with an eye to the Indians' own heritage.

On the whole, the commission's report was still the voice of the paternalistic non-Indian "expert," warning that the Indian would not be ready to run his affairs until he had faith in himself, suggesting that the Indians be "motivated" to participate in solving their problems, and urging that Indian ideas be sought, but adopted only when they were "workable"—as if the many programs imposed by the whites on the Indians had proved workable!

But the report was important because it articulated the beginning of an awareness by influential non-Indians that the Indians had a right to be different, that recognition of those differences should play a role in the creation of Indian programs, and that Indians who were familiar with the values and ideas of their own cultures, would know best what programs their people needed and would accept. Furthermore, the report came out firmly against termination without a tribe's consent, and in principle recommended allowing Indians ultimately to initiate their own programs and manage their own affairs, assuming responsibilities in the meantime "for different functions on a piecemeal basis"—an idea that was adopted by the Bureau of Indian Affairs in hesitant fashion about eight years later.

Following are several excerpts from the report.

The Indian himself should be the focus of all government policy affecting him. Money, land, education, and technical assistance are to be considered only as means to an end: on the one hand, that of restoring the Indian's pride of origin and faith in himself—a faith undermined by years of political and economic dependence on the Federal government; on the other, the arousing of a desire to share in the benefits of modern civilization. These are deeply human considerations. If neglected, they will defeat the best-intentioned of government plans.

To encourage pride in Indianness is not to turn back the clock. On the contrary, it is to recognize that the United States policy has hitherto failed to use this vital factor effectively as a force for assimilation and for enriching American culture. As a result, Indians who have already entered the dominant society have generally disdained their historic background, drawing away from it as though ashamed. Instead of serving as a bridge to enable others to move freely between the two worlds, they have too often interpreted their heritage imperfectly to the majority race and have proved useless in explaining their adopted culture to their own people. Only men who have a foot in each way of life and an appreciation of both can effectively lessen the gap which divides the two and thus cross-fertilize both.

No program from above can serve as a substitute for one willed by Indians themselves. Nor is their mere consent to a plan to be taken as sufficient. Such "consent" may be wholly passive, representing a submission to the inevitable, or it may be obtained without their full understanding or before they are either able or willing to shoulder unfamiliar responsibilities. What is essential is to elicit their own initiative and intelligent cooperation. . . .

An objective which should undergird all Indian policy is that the Indian individual, the Indian family, and the Indian community be motivated to participate in solving their own problems. The Indian must be given responsibility, must be afforded an opportunity he can utilize, and must develop faith in himself. Indian-made plans should receive preferential treatment, and, when workable, should be adopted. Government programs would be more effective if plans for education, health and economic development drew on those parts of the Indian heritage which are important not only to the Indians but also to the cultural enrichment of modern America. . . .

The Bureau's aim should be to let Indians conduct their own affairs as soon as possible without supervision. Accordingly, it should encourage their assumption of responsibilities for different functions on a piecemeal basis. Tribal land and resources should, however, remain under the Federal trust until the Indians, when able to hold and manage their property, decide otherwise.

DECLARATION OF INDIAN PURPOSE

American Indian Chicago Conference
June 13–20, 1961

As if to give the lie to paternalists who in 1961 believed that the Indians were still incapable of knowing what was best for them and still unmotivated to take the initiative in solving their own problems, some 420 Indians of 67 tribes gathered in June of that year in a history-making conference at the University of Chicago, where they voiced their opinions and desires on every aspect of contemporary Indian affairs.

For a week Indian committees met, assembled their thinking, and prepared resolutions and statements. The final drafts, including a great number of recommendations, were drawn up as a "Declaration of Indian Purpose" and passed by the entire conference.

The declaration began with the following resolution:

In order to give due recognition to certain basic philosophies by which the Indian people and all other people endeavor to live, We, the Indian people must be governed by high principles and laws in a democratic manner, with a right to choose our own way of life. Since our Indian culture is slowly being absorbed by the American society, we believe we have the responsibility of preserving our precious heritage; recognizing that certain changes are inevitable. We believe that the Indians should provide the adjustment and thus freely advance with dignity to a better life educationally, economically, and spiritually.

The resolution was followed by a statement of beliefs, presented as a Creed:

WE BELIEVE in the inherent right of all people to retain spiritual and cultural values, and that the free exercise of these values is necessary to the normal development of any people. Indians exercised this inherent right to live their own lives for thousands of years before the white man came and took their lands. It is a more complex world in which Indians live today, but the Indian people who first settled the New World and built the great civilizations which only now are being dug out of the past, long ago demonstrated that they could master complexity.

WE BELIEVE that the history and development of America show that the Indian has been subjected to duress, undue influence, unwarranted pressures, and policies which have produced uncertainty, frustration, and despair. Only when the public understands these conditions and is moved to take action toward the formulation and adoption of sound and consistent policies and programs will these destroying factors be removed and the Indian resume his normal growth and make his maximum contribution to modern society.

WE BELIEVE in the future of a greater America, an America which we were the first to love, where life, liberty, and the pursuit of happiness will be a reality. In such a future, with Indians and all other Americans cooperating, a cultural climate will be created in which the Indian people will grow and develop as members of a free society.

> The body of the declaration contained a host of proposals for policies and programs in such fields as resource and economic development, health, welfare, housing, education, law, relations between the tribes and the federal and state governments, and taxation. But as an authentic voice of the Indian, the declaration went further than any white man's document by making clear that the Indian wanted self-determination and the right to participate meaningfully in decisions that affected his life. He chafed under the heavy hand of the colonialist bureaucracy, which imposed programs on him that did not solve his problems, and he told the government specifically how he would like things to happen. In doing so, he underscored the fact that he had faith in himself, as well as the motivation and competency to solve his own problems.
>
> Following are several of the more pertinent sections of the declaration.

It has long been recognized that one Commissioner cannot give the personal attention to all tribal matters which they deserve. He cannot meet all callers to his office, make necessary visits to the field, and give full attention to the review of tribal programs and supporting budget requests. In view of these conditions, we most urgently recommend that the present organization of the Bureau of Indian Affairs be reviewed and that certain principles be considered no matter what the organizational change might be.

The basic principle involves the desire on the part of Indians to participate in developing their own programs with help and guidance as needed and requested, from a local decentralized technical and administrative staff, preferably located conveniently to the people it serves. . . . The Indians as responsible individual citizens, as responsible tribal representatives, and as responsible Tribal Councils want to participate, want to contribute to their own personal and tribal improvements and want to cooperate with their Government on how best to solve the many problems in a businesslike, efficient, and economical manner as rapidly as possible. . . .

We believe that where programs have failed in the past, the reasons were lack of Indian understanding, planning, participation, and approval.

A plan of development should be prepared by each Indian group, whose land or other assets are held in trust, whether such lands or assets are fully defined or not; such plans to be designed to bring about maximum utilization of physical resources by the dependent population and the development of that population to its full potential; such plans to be prepared by the Indians of the respective groups, with authority to call upon the agencies of the federal government for technical assistance, and the ultimate purpose of such planning to be the growth and development of the resources and the people;

That requests for annual appropriations of funds be based on the requirements for carrying into effect these individual development plans, including credit needs and capital investment, and the annual operating budget for the Bureau of Indian Affairs to include sufficient funds to cover the costs of preparing plans and estimates similar in operation to a Point IV plan.

That was in 1961. The philosophy inherent in the Indians' approach made no impact on the Bureau of Indian Affairs and had little practical response from the bureau for almost a decade.

THE HOPI WAY OF LIFE IS THE WAY OF PEACE

As Told by Andrew Hermequaftewa

The stirrings of Indians to regain freedom over their lives were accompanied by a revival of pride in their own traditions and an interest in traditionalist Indians who had kept alive the beliefs and life philosophies of their ancestors and preached a return to their fathers' lives of peace and purity. The movement was essentially a religious one, reflecting the revulsion that many Indians felt for the white man's present-day life and the lack of meaning Christianity had for them.

Among the best known of the traditionalist preachers, perhaps, are Thomas Banyacya, a Hopi, Oren Lyons, an Onondaga, and Wallace "Mad Bear" Anderson, a Tuscarora, but traditionalist leaders and groups have gathered support among tribes in all parts of the country. Each summer traditionalist leaders from different tribes travel together from one Indian center to another, discussing prophecies of their religion in National Aborigine conventions. Their faith in the ideas and ideals of their fathers has unified many Indians with a new devotion to their own traditions and a strength that flows from pride in their own backgrounds.

Many whites, too, have found inspiration in the beliefs of the traditionalists. The following talk by Andrew Hermequaftewa, the Bluebird Chief of the Hopi village of Shungopavi in Arizona, was recorded by Dr. Thomas B. Noble, Meredith Guillet, the superintendent of Walnut Canyon National Monument, and Platt Cline, secretary of the Arizona Commission of Indian Affairs, and was interpreted by Thomas Banyacya. It was printed as a pamphlet in 1954, and since then it has gone through a number of reprintings for a total of sixteen thousand copies. As a statement to Congress and the world, the Hopi patriarch recounted some Hopi traditions that are relevant to Indians and whites today.

Now will I begin from the very beginning of our traditional history of the Hopi.

Somewhere the human life began. There are many stories of this beginning. The Hopi believe that Maasau, the Great Spirit was the leader and the Creator of our land. With Him in the early beginning were the Spider Lady to keep the fire and her two nephews. These were the four of the beginning.

A long time has passed and there were other worlds and other peoples. We now are living today as descendants of people who were saved from the other world. Now, we call that the Underworld, because there the living stream changed from good into corruption. There were good people and they asked Maasau then for permission to come live with Him.

He was pleased because He had given the right of choice to them as human beings.

These good peaceful people from that earlier world were permitted to go live with Maasau. They became the first Hopi.

Maasau placed upon us, through them, the obligation to follow His way of life; being known by the works we do and by our promise never to abandon the good and peaceful way that would be HOPI.

The Hopi agreed to do what Maasau said and chose to live according to His way of life, and to follow His teachings. We made a vow that early day and we will never forsake it so long as we are Hopi. We were permitted then to come and live with Maasau.

We were welcome. We were taught the life plan of Maasau and were given instruction in the ways of His good living. After many days with Him, time came for all of the first Hopi to move out onto the face of this land. Maasau gathered us all about Him on that day and gave us instructions as to the obligations He placed upon us. He provided us with many altars and many emblems which, with us, are to represent the land and the people. These He placed in the hands of our leaders through whom we follow this new life.

After a day and night of praying and fasting, having heard the message from the Great Spirit, Maasau, all the Hopi assembled the next day at dawn to listen to His final message.

One certain clan out of all the group was appointed as leader-clan in our migration. An emblem was given them which represented the land and the people and the flowers of the earth. The leaders of this clan went through the sacred ceremony of initiation and their hair was washed. After this Maasau said, "Your name shall be 'Hopi.' I have given you this land and all these people under your care. This emblem I place in your hands. Following it, you will lead them along a good life as I have shown you. Always, you will continue to take care of all these people who are Hopi.

"You will be as their father. Take care of them as your children. Let them live a long life, a good life. Let there be plenty of rain. Let there be abundance of food for the children to eat. Let no one go hungry. Lead them always along the path of clean good harmonious life.

"Let your children grow into manhood and on into old age. Let there be so that when they go beyond this life they will be at peace; so that they will sleep in peace, so take care of them."

After this final speech of the Great Spirit, Maasau, our people began to move. They went to the different places where their instructions told.

The appointed leaders carried their altars with them. They carried food with which they would feed their children on the way. The planting stick, with which to put the corn deeply into the sand, they carried. There was a bag of tobacco which would be used for praying while they smoked. There was a jar of water for drinking. This is all the early Hopi had. There was no weapon of any kind.

They were to act as leaders to all people in the way of the peaceful life which Maasau had described to them. They were to be called "Hopi," therefore; because this means "Peaceful."

On the second day, when the people began to move again, a group was appointed to go ahead of all others. They were to be the eyes, the scouts, and show the way. And there were others appointed to follow after, to see that everything designated was taken along with them. So it is even today. I belong to that clan which was appointed to follow. It is the duty of the Bluebird Clan to follow all others. We watch for everything. We guard them along the life plan of Maasau.

So the first people moved on. The next day the ancestors

of us who follow went through every place the others had stayed, through their houses to look for anything that may have been lost or that may have been forgotten. After going through all the places the Bluebird Clan followed them one day behind, always; never with them. That was our duty then in the beginning, and that is what I am doing now.

I am carrying out the instructions by continuing these very duties that our forefathers were given by Maasau. Our traditional leaders who have moved on, who are ahead of us, have forgotten some things. We Bluebird Clan leaders are working to restore the good things that they have dropped, so that we keep all things given by Maasau. That is what I am doing now by bringing these words to you. I am the Bluebird Chief.

As the Hopi traveled from one place to another on their way, they carried food around their waists. During the many years of moving about they never took the food from about their waists because they were not going to stop permanently. They were on their way to a certain place. There was a sign given to them by Maasau. Whenever the Great Star appeared in the sky there the Hopi would settle for all time. Wherever they were then, there they were to take food from their waists and settle down to live.

Many Hopi had arrived around what is now the village of Shungopavi at the time the Great Star appeared in the sky. They stayed there and set about building homes. They had been instructed to build houses as high as four stories, which they did. Other people had scattered in all directions throughout the land. They had been given the same instructions, and so other villages came into being at the coming of the Great Star.

But many people of the other places began to forsake the life plan of Maasau. Their lives became corrupted. They began to practice warfare. Some of their leaders began to wonder what had become of the Hopi. They wanted to live the peaceful way of life of Maasau, and so they began to look for the true Hopi.

A Hopi will not molest anyone. He will not mistreat people.

We will live peacefully with all people. For this reason people began to come to Shungopavi, which was fully established as the first village. In this way, Shungopavi became the mother village to the Hopi.

Now when people came to Shungopavi leaders and asked permission to be admitted into the village, the traditional leaders would hold council and consider the question. The newcomers would be asked what could they do by way of helping the Hopi Way of life. The Bluebird Chief must ask them if they have any kind of weapons. All people must leave their weapons of destruction before they would be admitted into the Hopi Village.

Boastful people cannot become part of a Hopi Village. Only those who desire to live peacefully, to harm no one, are admitted into the religious order of the village life. Not all can be admitted. Many can, and many have been. Other villages have been established by those who were not admitted to Shungopavi and other villages have been established by people directly from Shungopavi. Here they would receive all their altars and their religious songs from the mother village. Because Maasau has told us to guard this land by this altar which was set up at Shungopavi, other villages have taken this flower to carry to their village. In this way, they want to live and carry on the duties of all the clan leaders as they were placed upon them by Maasau.

So was the pattern established through which all Hopi villages were built. It was all according to the instructions given by Maasau. The village leaders are appointed by the proper religious leaders from Shungopavi. They have the same obligations, duties, and authority as the leaders at Shungopavi. Nothing happened by chance. Everything was according to the dictates of Maasau. Village life was established, leaders were appointed, and different clans were given special duties. The land was being taken care of under the obligations of Maasau.

Our religious teachings are based upon the proper care of our land and the people who live upon it. We must not lose the way of life of our religion if we are to remain Hopis, The

Peaceful. We believe in that; we live it, day by day. We do not want to give it up for the way of another. For the benefit of our people throughout our land, for the people to come after us in our land, and for those who care to learn we Hopis want to be known among all other people throughout all other lands as the Hopi, the People of Peace. Let all people hear our voice.

People should not disregard each other. There should be respect for each other. The Great Spirit, Maasau, told our leaders that there would be trouble and confusion if we disregard His way. If the Hopi Way is followed, people may be able to settle all things in a proper way, since our way is based on the life plan of Maasau.

THE COMING OF BOHANNA

The Hopi lived among their villages a very long time. They worshipped Maasau at their altars and through their use of this land. There was peace. No man raised his hand in anger against another.

Then this person came to us from across the great water and from another land. We call him and his kind Bohanna, the white man. Maasau, being a Spirit, met the Bohanna as they came upon our shore.

The white man did not ask anyone for permission to come upon the land. Maasau spoke to him and said, "You should ask for permission to enter on this land. If you wish to come and live according to the way of the Hopi in this land and never abandon that way, you may. I will give you this new way of life and some of the land."

Maasau, being a Great Spirit, looked into the hearts of the Bohanna and knew that they had many things that they wanted to do in this land not according to the way of Maasau.

The white man asked Maasau if there were some people already occupying the land. Maasau said "Yes, their houses are already standing. There are villages already established. They have their fields, everything—their way of life."

Maasau, alone, can give this life and land according to the Hopi Way. He did so to the Hopis and all the peoples that came with them first, because they prayed for permission and followed the plan of life of Maasau. No other people should claim any part of this land, rightfully, therefore.

This is how the Hopi believe that their land is their own by right of gift from Maasau in the beginning. The Bohanna, the white man, was not given permission by Maasau to claim any part of the land of the Hopi.

Maasau has told our leaders that the Bohanna will try to get all this land and claim all of it for himself. He also told us that the leaders of the white men, who sent them across the waters, instructed them that they must respect all peoples they found living here. They must not mistreat us. They must not try to take things away from us. They must consult us on all things they wish to do with any part of this land. So the white men were instructed by their leaders, and so Maasau informed us, and so we Hopi have continued to live the good Way, the peaceful Hopi Way as given us by Maasau.

TODAY: HOPI AND BOHANNA

I tell you this of the traditional religion of the Hopi because the white man has another way of life. It changes constantly where the Hopi Way does not and has not since Maasau first showed us His way. We find much of the good in the way of the Bohanna, but we find it difficult to keep up with him in his search for change, or to understand all of his way of life. We prefer our unchanging Hopi Way. Hopi and Bohanna must respect each other.

Respect and understanding can come best through conference where each speaks in his own way. We, the leaders of the traditional Hopi, who are holding fast to our way of life, wish to have peace and happiness throughout all this land, and among all peoples. We want our way of life to continue on; for ourselves, for our children, and for their children who come after.

To live peacefully with all people has been an attempt that has taken us into many hard times. There have been many mistreatments at the hands of some of the Bohanna. I, the Bluebird Chief, have been punished where the Hopi Way and the way of the white man are not parallel. I have been in the white man's jail. Because I am Hopi, and because I hold to the way of Maasau. I have not struck back in any fashion at any time. This is according to the way of Maasau.

In the beginning, the Spaniards were among our villages 27 years. They became so corrupted that it seemed that their way of life was about to destroy the Hopi Way.

Later on, we know that you fought the Spaniard and cleared him from all this land. When that was done, there was a treaty in which the United States government agreed to respect the Hopi people. The United States government agreed to protect the Hopi and establish its boundaries: agreed to protect the Hopi resources. Unhappily for us now, there was included in that agreement the permission for the Secretary of the Interior to place other Indians upon Hopi land, when emergency needed. This has made the purpose of the agreements forgotten.

The Hopi land is the Hopi religion. The Hopi religion is bound up in the Hopi land. You have allowed the Navajo to surround us and use our land until the Hopi land has shrunk to a small part of that agreed upon by treaty.

The Hopi lives and protects his land by worshipping, by praying, by fasting, according to the plans and instructions of Maasau. He cannot raise his hand in anger against another. How then can he ever protect or take care of his land when the United States government is so strong and has taken so much of it to give to others? To this we have not agreed. We have not been consulted.

The white man should go to the proper Hopi leaders in all fairness and learn of the instructions from Maasau. The Bohanna can sit down in council with our leaders and learn the truths, if he wishes to do right. We, the few and the weaker, cannot come to you.

Many Hopi today, are disturbed and confused. It seems to them the white man disregards his promises and his agreements under which the Hopi land was set aside. The white man boasts he has full authority and power to do the things he wants to do. The teachings of the Great Maasau are the right way, for us; and we believe the United States government will see that if we have council. We know that if the right way is not followed, great evil will come to this land.

The leaders of the Bohanna in Washington have told us that if we accept this authority we will not lose our land. If we follow the policy of the white man we will have more power and more voice in our tribal affairs, so they say. Maasau warned us that when the white man came there would be many ways in which they would enforce their will upon the Hopi and change the Hopi Way of life.

The Hopi wants to continue in his way, follow his beliefs, and his religion. We are told that if we abandon these and follow the way of the Bohanna, or another, we will come to great disaster and will not continue to live with Maasau. There is certain punishment if we desert His way of life. For this reason the Hopi has always been taught to want to be a Hopi, a man of peace, and follow his own religion. He has been taught to hold fast to his land as given him by Maasau for as long as he lives in the way of Maasau.

We, the traditional leaders of the Hopi, ask that the leaders of the white man in Washington know that this is how we have taken care of our land and of our children. This, our religion, may be of benefit to other people, not Hopi, who may come after us if these matters are brought to all peoples. Let them hear our voice. We do not want to take part in a stage where we are simply disregarding each other. We should have respect for each other, for there is too much disregarding each other. We should have respect for each other, for there is too much good in all people for it to be lost.

It is true that many people are confused. They are troubled everywhere. This happening was foretold by Maasau. It would be a punishment for the Hopi if they leave this land. It is being taken from us now, so I am standing on my religious belief and all of the traditions of the Hopi when I ask you now to consider how we can regain our land as it was in the beginning.

The traditional leaders of the Hopi wish to ask some questions. Should the Bohanna force his way of life upon us without consulting us? Should our children be trained in the white man's way and not at all the Hopi Way? Do the white men wish to see the Hopi continue in their way of peace and happiness? How can you be sure that your way, new to us, can be better than the old way of the traditional Hopi? Can there be a better way than that of Maasau?

We were told that if we accept any other way of life we will so bring trouble upon ourselves. Our forefathers told us this, and their forefathers before them. Maasau told the first of the Hopi. We believe that if you continue with the present policy, our land will be gone and our way of life will be destroyed for this world. You, Bohanna, have marvelous inventions; but many of these seem to lead only to destruction of the Hopi way. Our leaders tell us that Maasau has warned against such a way of life that may lose for us this land, and destroy us as Hopi.

Many things were prophesied to us, and are being fulfilled today. If we foresake our Hopi religion the land will forsake us. There will be no more Hopi Way, no more Hopi people, no more peace. For a Hopi to try to live the white man's way is for him to desert the way of Maasau—and then he is gone from us as a Hopi.

Some young people, today, are in a position where they disregard everything we hold sacred; our religious life, our way of life in the villages, our meaningful ceremonies. We regret that some see the ceremonies as no more than curious spectacles, as the white man sees them.

That I may not be tiring to you, I ask that you in Washington consider all these facts and try to straighten out all problems by coming and talking with our leaders, the traditional leaders appointed by the traditional authorities. We then can go into all the prophecies and the things that the Hopi know as the way of life given to them by Maasau. So, I, the Bluebird Chief, ask you people, you leaders in Washington, and those who are interested in trying to find the peaceful way of life, to come to the Hopi for council talk with the Hopi leaders.

The young Hopi people who are being forced to go to war in other countries, contrary to all teachings of their religion, are disturbed beyond the understanding of most Bohannas.

Whoever causes a Hopi to raise his hand in war against another is not only harming the Hopi, but is also harming all other people. "Hopi" means "peaceful." That is our religion. That should be discussed.

This same thing took place in the other world before this one. The first Hopi escaped from that total destruction of life, by asking to follow and live with Maasau. He gave them permission to come and live with Him as peaceful people. We have vowed to adhere to that life. We are being forced to disregard everything that Maasau has told us. We are going after things, so that the young are not regarding traditional teachings. This is destruction beginning.

We, the Hopi leaders, want to sit with you and consider all these ancient teachings, the advice that has come to us from our forefathers, and the effects upon our way of life of the white man's power that is in Washington. We do not want to see the Hopi Way destroyed.

We believe that through an understanding, if you come and sit with us in council, we may save the Hopi Way of life. We may help save others from destruction by sharing our way of peace.

We know certain things will take place if we do not.

Therefore, I ask, as a Hopi, as the Bluebird Chief, will you in Washington who are in authority come and hold council with us? We would stop this loss of our land and destruction of what we have chosen as our way of life. We want to live as Hopis and worship the way we have been doing since the beginning. The Hopi religion, given to us by Maasau, is a way of peace that must be shared with all people. May we so share this with you? That is all.

AMERICAN INDIAN CAPITAL CONFERENCE ON POVERTY

A Statement Made for the Young People by Melvin Thom — May, 1964

In 1964 a momentous breakthrough occurred in Indian affairs. The Economic Opportunity Act, the major instrument of the Johnson administration's War on Poverty, included Indians as beneficiaries of the act's programs. For the first time, Indians were asked to propose and work out the plans for programs they wished to have on their reservations. Once the proposals had been approved, funds were made available to the Indians, who administered the programs themselves. At last Indians were permitted to take responsibility for the management of, and the handling of monies for, reservation programs, and on the whole they proved that they were, indeed, able to run their own affairs. Though this right was extended only to their management of Office of Economic Opportunity programs, the experience was not lost on the Indians. Almost at once it quickened their demand for similar rights over all government programs on the reservations, including those funded by the Bureau of Indian Affairs.

Up to the time of the Economic Opportunity Act, Indians had not usually been included as beneficiaries of legislation intended for the general population. Although they had benefited under the provisions of the Area Redevelopment Act, passed in the early days of the Kennedy administration, it was an exception. Indians, most congressmen felt, were cared for by the appropriations for the Bureau of Indian Affairs, and when the Economic Opportunity Act was first framed, it seemed likely that the Indians would be excluded from its provisions.

To convince official Washington that the Indians should be included in the act, a large American Indian Capital Conference on Poverty was convened in the Capital from May 9 to 12, 1964, when the legislation was still being written and debated. Several hundred Indians and as many non-Indians, gathered under the auspices of the Council on Indian Affairs, a federation of church groups and other Indian-interest organizations, visited congressmen and senators at the Capitol, held consultations with influential administration leaders, including Vice President Hubert Humphrey and Secretary of the Interior Stewart Udall, and won their point.

The conference was also notable because many young Indians, advocates of Red Power, showed up and for the first time demanded and gained the right to be heard by the older delegates. Near the close of the meeting their spokesman, Melvin Thom, a young Northern Paiute Indian from Walker River, Nevada, who was president of the National Indian Youth Council, stirred the conference with a statement "for the young people." Following are excerpts from his speech.

We are gathered here today to present the findings and recommendations of the poverty conditions which exist in our Indian homes. Poverty is nothing new to us. Many of us grew up in such conditions. We are joining in a concerted effort to remove the causes of poverty that destroys life among our people; this condition continues to eat away at our existence.

I would like to point out a little more about the basic Indian feeling toward the way he is being treated in regard to poverty. It is not easy to just sit down and make out a plan of action to remove poverty. It is not easy to even admit that we are poor. It is especially difficult for young people to say "We are poor —please help us." It is not easy to follow somebody always asking for help. The image of the American Indian is that of always asking. But the Indian youth fears this poverty and we have got to take a good look at what approach we are going to use to be rid of poverty.

The young people of the Indian tribes are going to be the ones to live with this, and sometime the Indian people are going to have to make a great effort—a concerted effort to remove poverty and the other conditions that have held the Indian people back from enjoying the comforts of life which we should be entitled to.

We as Indian youths know we cannot get away from the life which brought us here. To be an Indian is a very life to us and the conditions under which we live and the lives of our parents and relatives are affected. We cannot relax until this condition is removed; our conscience will never be clear until we have put forth effort to improve our conditions and the conditions of those at home.

We must recognize and point out to others that we do want to live under better conditions, but we want to remember that we are Indians. We want to remain Indian people. We want this country to know that our Indian lands and homes are precious to us. We never want to see them taken away from us.

As Indian youths we say to you today that the Indian cannot be pushed into the mainstream of American life. Our recognition as Indian people and Indian tribes is very dear to us. We cannot work to destroy our lives as Indian people. This will never serve the needs of the Indian people or this country.

Many of our friends feel that the Indian's greatest dream is to be free from second-class citizenship. We as youths have been taught that this freedom from second-class citizenship should be our goal. Let it be heard from Indian youth today that we do not want to be freed from our special relationship with the Federal Government. We only want our relationship between Indian Tribes and the Government to be one of good working relationship. We do not want to destroy our culture, our life that brought us through the period in which the Indians were almost annihilated.

We do not want to be pushed into the mainstream of American life. The Indian youth fears this, and this fear should be investigated and removed. We want it to be understood by all those concerned with Indian welfare that no people can ever develop when there is fear and anxiety. There is fear among our Indian people today that our tribal relationship with the Federal Government will be terminated soon. This fear must be removed and life allowed to develop by free choices. The policy to push Indians into the mainstream of American life must be re-evaluated. We must have hope. We must have a goal. But that is not what the Indian people want. We will never be able to fully join in on that effort.

For any program or policy to work we must be involved at the grassroots level. The responsibility to make decisions for ourselves must be placed in Indian hands. Any real help for Indian people must take cultural values into consideration. Programs set up to help people must fit into the cultural framework. . . .

We need to take a careful look at special programs. We need help for immediate plans and we also need to take into consideration the long-range policies and programs and where they are leading. What is needed at this time is a large national picture. The attitude that non-Indians, and some Indians, have is that someday the Indians are just going to disappear and that we should be working to make the Indians disappear is very wrong. We are not going to disappear. We have got to educate the American public and also our leaders that we are here to stay and that in staying here we have got to find a place for resolving our problems that will give us a life that has meaning for us and our Indian children and that there is a real hope that a complete life can be realized.

Indian tribes need greater political power to act. This country respects power and is based on the power system. If Indian communities and Indian tribes do not have political power we will never be able to hang on to what we have now. At the present time we have a right to own land—to exist as federal corporations—we have the self-building means to control this. There is a matter of putting that to work. We have a lot of communication to do. This communication has to come from the Indians themselves. We have got to get the message across. In the past our friends have taken it upon themselves to bring the message to the public and to the helping agencies. We have got to take a greater part in this role.

This conference is a good example of how we can work toward bringing our needs to the attention of the public and the helping agencies. The Indian youth should have an important role for he will be the one to be dealing with the benefits of the programs also. We must make an effort to achieve the goals of Indian people to act completely for themselves and a lot rests with the younger people. We have to stir up an interest among Indian youth that they have got to get together to make a concerted effort with our leading tribes and with the older Indian leadership.

We have to cooperate and learn to work together. The Indian youth have got to take this upon themselves because in many cases our older people do not have the means to communicate this message and too many of our young people have drifted off and gone into American cities and not served the Indians where they are needed. There is a great amount of work ahead for the Indians and their friends.

If the findings and recommendations of this conference can be realized we will have taken a big step in the way toward a better life for the Indian people. Maybe someday we will all look back and realize that at this conference the first big step was taken and how our future efforts were built on this work.

RESOLUTION FOR A NEW NATIONAL INDIAN POLICY

by Senator George McGovern
October 13, 1966

Senator George McGovern of South Dakota, a member of the Senate Indian Affairs Subcommittee and spokesman for a state that contains one of the largest Indian populations, was among the first figures of national influence to recognize the success of the Office of Economic Opportunity's approach to reservation programs and the resulting increase in the demand of Indians for self-determination in all their affairs.

Responding to these developments, McGovern introduced a resolution in the Senate in October, 1966, calling for a revised national Indian policy that among other things would make available to the reservations the services of other federal agencies, whose operating relations with the Indians would take a lesson from the OEO methods—that is, involve the Indians in the policy-making, control, and management of their programs.

McGovern's resolution died without action by the Congress. But its support of self-determination for the Indians showed the direction in which the wind was blowing. More Indians took heart at this first slim recognition in Washington that the time had come to end paternalism, and the voice of Indians demanding the right to run their own affairs grew stronger. In the Capital, in turn, the resolution and the Indians' support of it contributed a new sense of urgency to federal-Indian relations. Two governmental task forces, set up by President Johnson to study the status of Indian affairs and make recommendations to the White House, in 1967 headed long lists of programmatic suggestions with the exhortation that substantial Indian participation be involved at both national and reservation levels when any new proposals or programs were contemplated concerning improvement of Indian education, training, and employment or the economic development of Indian tribes. And on March 6, 1968, President Johnson himself led off a special Message to Congress on Indian Affairs with the words: "I propose a new goal for our Indian programs: A goal that ends the old debate about 'termination' of Indian programs and stresses self-determination; a goal that erases old attitudes of paternalism and promotes partnership self-help."

Time was to prove that this was little more than rhetoric, and that once again promises that would not be fulfilled were being made to the Indians. But McGovern's resolution had helped, at least, to accelerate the change of paternalistic attitudes long held by many whites in Washington.

Following are excerpts from Senator McGovern's speech that accompanied the introduction of his resolution in the Senate, and the resolution itself.

Our Indian policy since 1960 has turned in a favorable direction, and is now characterized by a wide range of constructive Federal programs and services available to Indian citizens. The tribal governing units established under the Indian Reorganization Act of 1934 constitute political entities through which these services have been organized into meaningful attacks on the chronic conditions of poverty in many Indian communities. The encouraging progress achieved through this approach must be maintained and accelerated so that all Indians may share in the great social and economic advancements of our Nation.

I consider it crucial that we in Congress adopt a new National Indian Policy Statement at this time to demonstrate to Indian people and other citizens the seriousness of our desire to continue development of programs and services that will assure solution to the long-standing problems of Indians. By setting forth with clarity the perimeters of our Indian policy, it will be possible to hold the Executive agencies accountable for their work in Indian communities. A sound and constructive Indian policy statement from the Congress will support President Johnson's firm instructions to the Commissioner of Indian Affairs to put the first Americans first on our agenda. And finally, a new Indian policy will assure us of greater participation and cooperation from the Indians themselves in the government's efforts to improve their well-being.

For a new Indian policy to be truly effective, it must reflect certain favorable characteristics that I want to offer for your consideration.

1. *Self-Determination.* I believe the foremost characteristic of our Indian policy should be self-determination for the people it serves. Too often in the past the Federal Government has done what it has thought best for Indians, with minor regard for the hopes and aspirations of the Indians.

Many of our foreign aid endeavors are predicated on the principle that disadvantaged people will respond more readily to constructive programs when they participate in planning objectives and goals. Certainly we can afford to do no less for the first citizens of this nation.

We should insist that reservation development plans be worked from the "grass roots" level upward, rather than evolving as creatures of Washington superimposed on reservations with little or no Indian involvement.

Instead of constantly espousing the attributes of "mainstream" society to Indian people, we should offer the programs and services that will permit the growth of a healthy and productive individual. When this is successfully accomplished, the Indian can then determine his own "mainstream," which may be in urban America or in a useful capacity on his home reservation.

2. *Self-Help.* The second most desirable characteristic of our Indian policy should be self-help. The tribal groups who have been motivated to assume this trait have shown growth and progress toward self-sufficiency. I believe that great care must be exercised by program administrators to devise ways in which the tribal groups may demonstrate self-help in order to achieve maximum benefits from programs.

No program should be conceived that does not make provisions for tribes to exercise this important trait. Admittedly, some few tribes still harbor deep resentment and suspicion toward the Federal Government and experience difficulty in working with them cooperatively; in these instances Federal officials will be challenged to administer their programs in a manner to motivate greater effort by the Indians.

3. *Consistency.* Perhaps at no other time in history is there

a more paramount need for a constructive and consistent Indian policy. All areas of Indian living when compared to the general population are so sub-standard they almost defy comprehension. It is inconceivable that during our country's period of low unemployment that excessive unemployment rates are commonly accepted on many reservations. And regrettably, rates of 90 per cent unemployment can still be found on some Indian reservations in the world's richest nation. . . .

There will be those who urge relocation, termination and other schemes to solve Indian problems. But these approaches in the past have only retarded progress.

It is possible that some tribes may be considered capable of assuming full responsibility for their affairs. When such developments occur, then orderly plans should be developed to relieve the Federal Government of further responsibility for their welfare. When tribes petition to end their special Federal relationship, they should, of course, be given that opportunity.

But I will oppose any general arbitrary policy of termination for the groups whose social and economic conditions require long-range Federal assistance.

4. *Adequacy.* Indian needs are no longer responsive to the "one to one" approach between them and the Bureau of Indian Affairs. To effectively engage in an all-out war against poverty on reservations, the services of other government agencies, as well as Indian participation, will be required. Therefore, the proper balance of programs must be directed to the problems of Indians to realize success. This will require more than a modest investment of Federal appropriations. . . .

For our Indian policy to be truly effective and support the wide variety of programs that will enable us to strike at the very heart of the social ills that retard Indian progress, we must be prepared to appropriate increasing sums of money in the years ahead.

5. *Innovation.* Because the Office of Economic Opportunity was willing to offer Indian people new and innovative approaches in the planning, implementation and administration

of its varied programs, that agency has enjoyed unusual success in its work on reservations. It is my belief that OEO has set new program standards for other agencies to follow in working with Indian people.

No longer will tribal leaders and rank and file members be satisfied with Federal officials who do not offer them similar experiences in program development. As I stated earlier, Indian people are striving for their rightful share of responsibility in efforts designed to improve their welfare. The Office of Economic Opportunity has helped to ignite this spark of enthusiasm, and I am hopeful the other agencies will capitalize on it in the conduct of their programs. . . .

I believe that many tribal groups have developed their capabilities to a level where government agencies should consider arrangements whereby contracts would be established with tribal governing units to allow them to administer programs in whole or part. If additional legislative authority is required by the agencies to accommodate this approach, they should submit such proposals to the Congress for consideration.

CONCURRENT RESOLUTION
NATIONAL AMERICAN INDIANS AND
ALASKA NATIVES POLICY RESOLUTION

Resolved by the Senate (the House of Representatives concurring),

Whereas it is recognized by Congress that American Indians and Alaska Natives (Eskimos, Indians and Aleuts) suffer from adverse economic, health, education and social conditions which prevent them from sharing equally in the great social and economic advancements achieved by our Nation; and

Whereas it is the understanding of Congress that periodic reversals in our Government's Indian policy throughout the years have ruled against full development of the human and economic potential of Indian communities, thus prolonging the aforementioned deplorable conditions; and

Whereas improved and expanded services in Indian communities in recent years through direct Federal Indian service programs and a wide variety of other services have begun accomplishing encouraging breakthroughs; Now, therefore, be it

Resolved by the Senate (the House of Representatives concurring), That it is the sense of the Congress that—

(1) the deplorable conditions of American Indians and Alaska Natives can only be alleviated through a sustained, positive and dynamic Indian policy with the necessary constructive programs and services directed to the governing bodies of these groups for application in their respective communities, offering self-determination and self-help features for the people involved; and that our Government's concern for its Indian citizens be formalized in a new National Indian Policy so that the beneficial effects may be continued until the day when the Nation's moral and legal obligations to its first citizens—the American Indians—are fulfilled.

(2) modern day needs of Indian people are no longer responsive to the programs and services of the two major Federal Indian Service Agencies alone (the Bureau of Indian Affairs and the Division of Indian Health), but the complete solution of Indian problems will require new and innovative services for the full development of Indian and Alaska Native people and their communities, and that the Bureau of Indian Affairs, because of its traditional role in the Indian field, access to important records, and direct relationships with tribal officials, should be charged with the important responsibility of coordinating the wide range of Federal, State and local resources.

(3) Indian and Alaska Native governing bodies should be recognized as having the full authority to determine the extent and manner of utilizing all available resources for their communities.

(4) American Indian and Alaska Native property will be protected; that Indian culture and identity will be respected; that the necessary technical guidance and assistance will be given to insure future economic independence; that continued efforts will be directed to maximum development of natural

resources; that inadequate and substandard housing and sanitation will be corrected; that a comprehensive health program incorporating and assuring curative and preventive physical and mental health will be further developed for Indian and Alaska Natives; and that a long-term general, vocational, technical and professional education program will be encouraged and developed for both old and young American Indians and Alaska Natives so that they may share fully in our society;

(5) the Secretary of Interior should periodically review all the activities of the Commissioner and Bureau of Indian Affairs to assure Congress of maximum utilization of Federal, State and local resources for Indian and Alaska Native well-being; and that the Secretary should submit an annual report with necessary legislative recommendations to Congress to indicate the manner in which the intent of this resolution is being carried out; and

(6) American Indian and Alaska Native communities should be given the freedom and encouragement to develop their maximum potential; and that Congress will support a policy of developing the necessary programs and services to bring Indians and Alaska Natives to a desirable social and economic level of full participating citizens.

INDIAN STATEMENT ON POLICY AND LEGISLATION

Washington, D.C., February 2, 1967

Despite the Johnson administration's assurance that it would further Indian self-determination, action did not follow the words. In 1966 and 1967 Interior Department officials prepared a so-called omnibus bill of new economic legislation for presentation to Congress as an Indian Resources Development Act. While the bill was being drafted by department "experts," Commissioner of Indian Affairs Robert Bennett, himself an Oneida Indian, and various department officials met with Indian spokesmen at hearings around the nation, supposedly to learn what kind of legislation the tribes wanted. Although no inkling was given the Indians that the bill was already being written in Washington, a tentative draft of it came into their hands during the course of the hearings.

Realization of the new deception, plus the fact that the draft did not reflect what the Indians considered to be their true needs and desires, angered them. Despite their protests, the Department of the Interior, still not trusting the competency of the Indians to know what was good for them and continuing to impose its own ideas on them, readied a final draft of the bill for Congress.

In February, 1967, a large group of Indians, called together in Washington to give their approval to the bill, instead voiced their opposition to it. Although some of its provisions seemed acceptable, the bill included many proposals that stirred new fears and bitterness among the Indians. They missed most of all a commitment by the administration to repudiate the hated 1953 congressional termination resolution, which still hung threateningly over their tribes, and they divided on how harshly to express their disapproval. A final, somewhat mild statement, sent by the group to President Johnson on February 2 and signed by the conference leaders, Norman Hollow, Earl Old Person, and Roger Jourdain, merely pointed out objections to certain portions of the bill and asked for more time for the tribes to consider the entire draft.

In the end Congress, recognizing the Indians' opposition to the measure, ignored it, and the so-called omnibus bill died ignominiously. In retrospect, the Indians' study and disapproval of the bill, as reflected in their Washington conference's February, 1967, statement to the President, were a significant step along the road of asserting control over policies that would affect them.

Following are excerpts from their statement.

Dear Mr. President:

Upon presentation of and analysis by the delegates of this legislation, certain major titles and provisions thereof were rigorously opposed and unanimously rejected upon the grounds that they are inimical to, and uncongruous with, the present needs, capabilities and conditions of the American Indians. Implementation of certain of the managerial techniques of the proposed legislation affecting mortgage, hypothecation and sale of Indian lands, would render the Indian people immediately vulnerable to subversive economic forces, leading inevitably and inalterably to the prompt erosion and demise of the social and economic culture of the American Indian.

Enactment of this legislation by the Congress would constitute a breach of the trust comprehended under original Indian treaties, if not in word, then in the spirit of the same. . . .

For other citizens government exists to serve them—as a matter of right and not of favor. It is time that government consistently recognize that it is our servant and not our master. Many of our difficulties today, we feel, lie in the unresponsiveness of public officials to our social and economic needs, despite the fact that adequate legislation exists to further Indian progress in many fields. The last major progressive policy and legislation was adopted in 1934—33 years ago. Today, we need a revision and updating of that policy. That policy saved our lands, insured our rights of limited self-government, and opened the door to financial credit for Indians.

Today, we need a reaffirmation of our rights to continue to occupy the lands remaining to us. Our very existence as a people is dependent on our lands. The tax status of Indian lands is founded on agreement by the Indians and the United States. This immunity is recognition that the Indian people paid more than adequate consideration when they gave up valuable land in exchange for smaller, less valuable parcels — today occupied by some 300,000 to 500,000 Indians.

Today, we are faced with threats of termination. We ask you to seek the repudiation of the ideas behind Concurrent Resolution 108, adopted in 1953. . . .

Mr. President, we wish to cooperate. With your understanding and consideration we will succeed. . . .

Respectfully submitted,
Chairman, Norman Hollow
Co-chairman, Earl Old Person
Co-chairman, Roger Jourdain

"WE ARE NOT FREE"

Testimony of Clyde Warrior, President, National Indian Youth Council February 2, 1967

In general, in the late 1960's the most articulate and insistent arguments for Indian self-determination were made by young, college-educated Indians. They were a new generation, proud of their Indian heritage, unwilling to share their fathers' acceptance of white paternalism, and contemptuous of the society of the white man, which everywhere around them seemed to be falling into disarray.

Increasingly they appeared at university seminars, at meetings of national organizations, and at hearings of government agencies whose affairs touched Indian life. Their speeches and testimony, essentially demands for self-determination for Indians, comprised simultaneous attacks on many fronts: on the colonialist bureaucrats and white "Indian experts"; on their own "red apple" (red on the outside and white on the inside) elders and tribal leaders; and on the collusion between self-seeking or fearful Indians and whites that continued to keep control and power in the hands of the Indians' oppressors.

On February 2, 1967, the same day that older Indians in Washington were presenting President Johnson with a cautious reproof of the administration's proposed "omnibus bill," Clyde Warrior, an eloquent young Ponca Indian from eastern Oklahoma who had become president of the National Indian Youth Council, testified at a hearing of the President's National Advisory Commission on Rural Poverty in Memphis, Tennessee. His statement is typical of many utterances and writings that made him almost a legendary hero to young Indians throughout the country even before his untimely death in 1968. It is a moving plea for Indian freedom, and at its heart is a perceptive linking of Indian poverty with the white man's continuing unwillingness to allow Indians to run their own affairs. White bureaucrats and "experts" from both government and private (university, foundation, church, state and local political and business) sectors of the country were moving in authoritatively on the control and management of government-funded antipoverty programs. The trend was undermining the Indian self-government aspects of those projects that had seemed so promising during the first days of the OEO and threatening to negate a similar potential for self-government, envisioned by Senator

McGovern, in the operation of other governmental agency programs that would come to the reservations. Warrior's statement reflects this development.

His theme, the major thrust of many of his speeches, struck a responsive chord among young Indians: tribal leaders had to recognize that white "experts" could not end poverty or solve other problems on the reservations; only "the poor, the dispossessed, the Indians" could decide what was best for them.

Following is the principal portion of his presentation to the commission.

M ost members of the National Indian Youth Council can remember when we were children and spent many hours at the feet of our grandfathers listening to stories of the time when the Indians were a great people, when we were free, when we were rich, when we lived the good life. At the same time we heard stories of droughts, famines and pestilence. It was only recently that we realized that there was surely great material deprivation in those days, but that our old people felt rich because they were free. They were rich in things of the spirit, but if there is one thing that characterizes Indian life today it is poverty of the spirit. We still have human passions and depth of feeling (which may be something rare in these days), but we are poor in spirit because we are not free—free in the most basic sense of the word. We are not allowed to make those basic human choices and decisions about our personal life and about the destiny of our communities which is the mark of free mature people. We sit on our front porches or in our yards, and the world and our lives in it pass us by without our desires or aspirations having any effect.

We are not free. We do not make choices. Our choices are made for us; we are the poor. For those of us who live on reservations these choices and decisions are made by federal administrators, bureaucrats, and their "yes men," euphemistically called tribal governments. Those of us who live in non-reservation areas have our lives controlled by local white power elites. We have many rulers. They are called social workers, "cops," school teachers, churches, etc., and now

84

OEO employees. They call us into meetings to tell us what is good for us and how they've programmed us, or they come into our homes to instruct us and their manners are not always what one would call polite by Indian standards or perhaps by any standards. We are rarely accorded respect as fellow human beings. Our children come home from school to us with shame in their hearts and a sneer on their lips for their home and parents. We are the "poverty problem" and that is true; and perhaps it is also true that our lack of reasonable choices, our lack of freedoms, our poverty of spirit is not unconnected with our material poverty.

The National Indian Youth Council realizes there is a great struggle going on in America now between those who want more "local" control of programs and those who would keep the power and the purse strings in the hands of the federal government. We are unconcerned with that struggle because we know that no one is arguing that the dispossessed, the poor, be given any control over their own destiny. The local white power elites who protest the loudest against federal control are the very ones who would keep us poor in spirit and worldly goods in order to enhance their own personal and economic station in the world.

Nor have those of us on reservations fared any better under the paternalistic control of federal administrations. In fact, we shudder at the specter of what seems to be the forming alliances in Indian areas between federal administrators and local elites. Some of us fear that this is the shape of things to come in the War on Poverty effort. Certainly, it is in those areas where such an alliance is taking place that the poverty program seems to be "working well." That is to say, it is in those areas of the country where the federal government is getting the least "static" and where federal money is being used to bolster the local power structure and local institutions. By "everybody being satisfied," I mean the people who count and the Indian or poor does not count.

Let us take the Head Start Program as an instance. We are told in the not-so-subtle racist vocabulary of the modern middle class that our children are "deprived." Exactly what they are deprived of seems to be unstated. We give our children love, warmth and respect in our homes and the qualities necessary to be a warm human being. Perhaps many of them get into trouble in their teens because we have given them too much warmth, love, passion, and respect. Perhaps they have a hard time reconciling themselves to being a number on an IBM card. Nevertheless, many educators and politicians seem to assume that we, the poor, the Indians, are not capable of handling our own affairs and even raising our own children and that state institutions must do that job for us and take them away from us as soon as they can. My grandmother said last week, "Train your child well now for soon she will belong to her teacher and the schools." Many of our fears about the Head Start Program which we had from listening to the vocabulary of educators and their intentions were not justified, however. In our rural areas the program seems to have turned out to be just a federally subsidized kindergarten which no one seems to take too seriously. It has not turned out to be, as we feared, an attempt to "re-thread" the "twisted head" of the child from a poor home. Head Start, as a program, may not have fulfilled the expectations of elitist educators in our educational colleges, and the poor may not be ecstatic over the results, but local powers are overjoyed. This is the one program which has not upset any one's apple cart and which has strengthened local institutions in an acceptable manner, acceptable at least to our local "patrons."

Fifty years ago the federal government came into our communities and by force carried most of our children away to distant boarding schools. My father and many of my generation lived their childhoods in an almost prison-like atmosphere. Many returned unable even to speak their own language. Some returned to become drunks. Most of them had become white haters or that most pathetic of all modern Indians—Indian haters. Very few ever became more than very confused, ambivalent and immobilized individuals —never able to reconcile the tensions and contradictions built inside themselves by outside institutions. As you can imagine, we have little faith in such kinds of federal programs devised for our betterment nor do we see education as a panacea for all ills. In recent days, however, some of us have been thinking that perhaps the damage done to our communities by forced assimilation and directed acculturative programs was minor compared to the situation in which our children now find themselves. There is a whole generation of Indian children who are growing up in the American school system. They still look to their relatives, my generation, and my father's to see if they are worthy people. But their judgment and definition of what is worthy is now the judgment most Americans make. They judge worthiness as competence and competence as worthiness. And I am afraid me and my fathers do not fare well in the light of this situation and judgment. Our children are learning that their people are not worthy and thus that they individually are not worthy. Even if by some stroke of good fortune, prosperity was handed to us "on a platter" that still would not soften the negative judgment our youngsters have of their people and themselves. As you know, people who feel themselves to be unworthy and feel they cannot escape this unworthiness turn to drink and crime and self-destructive acts. Unless there is some way that we as Indian individuals and communities can prove ourselves competent and worthy in the eyes of our youngsters there will be a generation of Indians grow to adulthood whose reaction to their situation will make previous social ills seem like a Sunday School picnic.

For the sake of our children, for the sake of the spiritual and material well-being of our total community we must be able to demonstrate competence to ourselves. For the sake of our psychic stability as well as our physical well-being we must be free men and exercise free choices. We must make decisions about our own destinies. We must be able to learn and profit by our own mistakes. Only then can we become competent and prosperous communities. We must be free in the most literal sense of the word—not sold or coerced into accepting programs for our own good, not of our own making or choice. Too much of what passes for "grassroots democracy" on the American scene is really a slick job of salesmanship. It is not hard for sophisticated administrators to sell tinsel and glitter programs to simple people—programs which are not theirs, which they do not understand and which cannot but ultimately fail and contribute to already strong feelings of inadequacy. Community development must be just what the word implies, Community Development. It cannot be packaged programs wheeled into Indian communities by outsiders which Indians can "buy" or once again brand themselves as unprogressive if they do not "cooperate." Even the best of outside programs suffer from one very large defect — if the program falters helpful outsiders too often step in to smooth over the rough spots. At that point any program ceases to belong to the people involved and ceases to be a learning experience for them. Programs must be Indian creations, Indian choices, Indian experiences. Even the failures must be Indian experiences because only then will Indians understand why a program failed and not blame themselves for some personal inadequacy. A better program built upon the failure of an old program is the path of progress. But to achieve this experience, competence, worthiness, sense of achievement and the resultant material prosperity Indians must have the responsibility in the ultimate sense of the word. Indians must be free in the sense that other more prosperous Americans are free. Freedom and prosperity are different sides of the same coin and there can be no freedom without complete responsibility. And I do not mean the fictional responsibility and democracy of passive consumers of programs; programs which emanate from and whose responsibility for success rests in the hands of outsiders — be they federal administrators or local white elitist groups.

Many of our young people are captivated by the lure of the American city with its excitement and promise of unlimited opportunity. But even if educated they come from powerless and inexperienced communities and many times carry with them a strong sense of unworthiness. For many of them the promise of opportunity ends in the gutter on the skid rows of Los Angeles and Chicago. They should and must be given a better chance to take advantage of the opportunities they have. They must grow up in a decent community with a strong sense of personal adequacy and competence.

America cannot afford to have whole areas and communities of people in such dire social and economic circumstances. Not only for her economic well-being but for her moral well-being as well. America has given a great social and moral message to the world and demonstrated (perhaps not forcefully enough) that freedom and responsibility as an ethic is inseparable from and, in fact, the "cause" of the fabulous American standard of living. America has not however been diligent enough in promulgating this philosophy within her own borders. American Indians need to be given this freedom and responsibility which most Americans assume as their birth right. Only then will poverty and powerlessness cease to hang like the sword of Damocles over our heads stifling us. Only then can we enjoy the fruits of the American system and become participating citizens — Indian Americans rather than American Indians.

Perhaps, the National Indian Youth Council's real criticism is against a structure created by bureaucratic administrators who are caught in this American myth that all people assimilate into American society, that economics dictates assimilation and integration. From the experience of the National Indian Youth Council, and in reality, we cannot emphasize and recommend strongly enough the fact that no one integrates and disappears into American society. What ethnic groups do is not integrate into American society and economy individually, but enter into the mainstream of American society as a people, and in particular as communities of people. The solution to Indian poverty is not "government programs" but in the competence of the person and his people. The real solution to poverty is encouraging the competence of the community as a whole.

[The] National Indian Youth Council recommends for "openers" that to really give these people "the poor, the dispossessed, the Indians," complete freedom and responsibility is to let it become a reality not a much-heard-about dream and let the poor decide for once, what is best for themselves. . . .

"I AM A YAKIMA AND CHEROKEE INDIAN, AND A MAN"

Statement of Sidney Mills
October 13, 1968

Even with freedom and self-determination, the Indians' hope and promise of being able to solve their social and economic problems and create satisfying lives for themselves rest on the protection of their lands and resources and the observance of rights guaranteed them by federal treaties. Yet they have never been free of the pressures of white men to take from them what they possess, and their fight for freedom has often been two-edged: for self-determination, and in defense of their lands and rights.

The crushing of the Plains tribes in the latter part of the nineteenth century ended the ability of the Indians to defend themselves by military means. Since then they have had to rely—though with only occasional success—on the law courts and public opinion. Despite appeals to both avenues, tribe after tribe has continued to lose land, water, and other resources to non-Indians in the twentieth century. In recent years the Supreme Court permitted the Army Engineers to break the nation's oldest existing treaty and turn the most productive portion of the New York State Senecas' Allegany Reservation into a reservoir. In the Dakotas and elsewhere other reservations were similarly gutted by dam builders. In the arid West and Southwest water has been diverted away from Indian lands and channeled instead to non-Indian irrigation farmers and other white users. Most hunting grounds and fishing stations were destroyed long ago; where they still exist, even though they are no longer as productive as they formerly were, their use by Indians according to their treaty rights has been opposed, curtailed, hung with regulations and hobbling legal harassments, and even halted.

The erosion of the Indians' assets and rights is a continuation of the story that began with the near-extermination of the buffalo as a means to end the Indians' existence as Indians. Each loss reduces the Indians' opportunity to achieve economic self-sufficiency, sets them back, and helps to perpetuate their poverty and helplessness. But the loss often has other measurements as well. Land, water, fish, and other resources have enormous significances, sacred and otherwise, that sustain the spiritual strength of various Indian peoples. The earth is the mother to many tribes; it cannot be sold. When it is wrenched away the Indian and his group are sapped, if not destroyed.

In the Northwest, since long before the white men came, fish have been not only the principal food for numerous tribes, but an integral ingredient of the rounds of their ceremonies and daily life. Without the ability to fish, the Indian almost ceases to be. That fact, recognized in treaties made with the tribes in the 1850's guaranteeing them certain continued fishing rights, has little meaning to the present-day white man. Dams, pollution, and excessive commercial fishing have depleted the fish in many of the rivers of the Northwest; as a result, there are strict conservation laws, which the officials of Washington, Oregon, and Idaho have attempted to apply to Indians as well as whites. Since the conservation laws conflict with the treaty rights, the Indians have resisted them, claiming that they have always been conservation-minded themselves, that they were not the cause of the fish depletion, that they take such a small percentage of the annual catch as compared with whites that there is no need for the breaking of their treaties—and that the states, anyway, have no right to break the treaties.

The conflict, centered principally on the rivers around Puget Sound and on the middle Columbia, increased in intensity and violence during the 1960's. Numerous arrests of Indians and court cases failed to settle the issue. The spectacle of fights in boats between state officials and Indian men, women, and children, of armed Indians standing guard over their fishermen, and of the bulldozing of an Indian fishing camp evoked memories of nineteenth-century Indian wars of resistance. Furthermore, the dramatic confrontations, highlighted by the courage of outnumbered Indian families standing up to the white "power structure," gave a new hue to the Indians' struggle for freedom throughout the nation. Indians elsewhere, particularly the young, watched and were inspired. The northwestern states were trying to break treaties that the tribes had made with the federal government. They had no right to do so, and the federal government should have protected the tribes' treaties against the states. Its efforts against the states, however, were feeble at best. Therefore, if the federal government would not go all out to protect the Indians' treaty rights, the Indians would have to do so themselves, even if it meant having to resort to activist defensive measures. The bitterness of confrontation and active defense, smoldering first over fishing rights in the Northwest, began to spread. By 1970 the attempts at persuasive arguing were giving way to militant action by Indians in many parts of the country.

The following statement by Sidney Mills, the son of a Yakima and a Cherokee, and an enrolled member of the Yakima tribe of Washington, reflects the growth and extent of the bitterness of Indians fighting for their rights. Mills was a Pfc in the American Army when he drafted the statement on October 13, 1968, after a series of violent clashes between Indian fishermen and Washington state officials in the Northwest.

I am Yakima and Cherokee Indian, and a man. For two years and four months, I've been a soldier in the United States Army. I served in combat in Vietnam — until critically wounded. I recently made a decision and publicly declare it today — a decision of conscience, of commitment and allegiance.

I owe and swear first allegiance to Indian people in the sovereign rights of our many Tribes. Owing to this allegiance and the commitment it now draws me to, I HEREBY RENOUNCE FURTHER OBLIGATION IN SERVICE OR DUTY TO THE UNITED STATES ARMY.

My first obligation now lies with the Indian people fighting for the lawful Treaty Right to fish in usual and accustomed waters of the Nisqually, Columbia and other Rivers of the Pacific Northwest, and in serving them in this fight in any way possible.

Anyone fully aware of the facts and issues involved in this fight can understand that my decision is not difficult. What is difficult to understand is why these United States, and the State of Washington in particular, make it necessary for such decisions to be made. Why do the United States and the State of Washington command me to such a decision by their actions in seeking to effectively destroy the Indian people of this State and our way of life by denying rights that are essential to our existence?

This fight is real — as is the threat to Indian existence under the enforced policy objectives of the State of Washington, as permitted by the compromised position and abdication of responsibilities by the U.S. Government.

The defense of Indian people and a chosen way of life in this fight for unrelinquished fishing rights is more compelling and more demanding of my time and commitment than any duty to the U.S. military. I renounce, and no longer consider myself under, the authorities and jurisdiction of the U.S. Army.

I have served the United States in a less compelling struggle in Vietnam and will not be restricted from doing less for my people within the United States. The U.S. would have accepted sacrifice of my life in Vietnam in a less legitimate cause—in fact, nearly secured such sacrifice and would have honored such death. Yet I have my life and am now prepared to stand in another battle, a cause to which the United States owes its protection, a fight for people who the United States has instead abandoned. My action is taken with the knowledge that the Nation that would have accepted an honored death by its requirement may now offer only severe consequence and punishment because I now choose to commit my life to Indian people. I have given enough to the U.S. Army—I choose now to serve my people.

My decision is influenced by the fact that we have already buried Indian fishermen returned dead from Vietnam, while Indian fishermen live here without protection and under steady attack from the power processes of this Nation and the States of Washington and Oregon. I note that less than a month ago, we counted the death of another Indian fisherman, Jimmy Alexander, because of the conditions imposed upon our people to secure a livelihood while avoiding arrest. These conditions continued off Cook's Landing on the Columbia River, where Jimmy drowned, largely because the President of the United States ignored a direct appeal to intervene in the arrest case of Army Sergeant Richard Sohappy, a friend and fellow fisherman of Jimmy Alexander.

Sergeant Sohappy is back in Vietnam on his third tour of duty there. He was arrested three times in June for illegal net fishing, while home on recuperative furlough recovering from his fourth series of combat wounds and while attempting to secure income for his large family. For his stand in Vietnam, this Nation awarded him a Silver Star and Bronze Star, among others. For fighting for his family and people, this Nation permitted a professional barber acting as Justice of the Peace to interpret his Treaty, to ignore his rights, and to impose punishment and record under criminal conviction. His Commander-in-Chief, Lyndon Johnson, routinely referred the appeal for intervention to the Department of Interior, which routinely refused to act on basis of false information and facts—and on basis of a presumption of guilt on the part of Sergeant Sohappy. He now continues to fight for this Nation in Vietnam, his fellow Yakima tribesman Jimmy Alexander is dead, and the United States stands indifferent while his people and their rights are destroyed.

Equally, I have been influenced by the fact that many Indian women and children have become obligated by conditions and necessity to sustain a major burden in this fight. These women and children have sustained some of the most brutal and mercenary attacks upon their lives and persons that have been suffered by any Indian people since prior Indian wars.

Just three years ago today, on October 13, 1965, 19 women and children were brutalized by more than 45 armed agents of the State of Washington at Frank's Landing on the Nisqually River in a vicious, unwarranted attack. It is not that this is the anniversary of that occasion that brings us here or which prompts my declaration on this day—but rather the fact that such actions have gained a frequency in occurrence and have come to be an everyday expectation in their lives. As recently as last night, we have witnessed the beating or injury of women simply because they are among the limited numbers who will not surrender our limited rights.

This consideration, as much as any, gives immediacy to my decision and prompts me to act upon it now. I will not be among those who draw pride from a past in which I had no part nor from a proud heritage I will not uphold. We must give of ourselves today—and I will not be content to have women or children fighting in my stead. At the least, I will be among them—at the least, they will not be alone.

The disturbing question is, "Why must our Indian people fight?"

Why can't an Al Bridges or Lewis Squally fish on the Nisqually without placing their lives and property in jeopardy, when 45,000 non-Indian citizens of this State draw their income from the commercial salmon industry? Why can't a Bob Satiacum or Frankie Mounts continue their ancestral way of life in fishing, when 500,000 sports fishermen pleasure themselves upon this resource? Why must the life patterns of a Richard Sohappy be altered and the subsistence of a family be denied, when two to three times the total annual salmon

catch by Indians of this State are alone escaping past Bonne-
ville Dam and as many being caught by non-Indians below
it? Why must a Jimmy Alexander lose his life under unnatural
conditions, when non-Indians were able to catch 11,000,000
salmon to the Indians' half million in the last year before
restrictions were enforceably imposed upon my people?

Is it because the U.S. Constitution, which declares all
Treaties made to be the Supreme Law of the Land and contradictory state laws void, is almost 200 years old? But treaties
are still being made under force of that document. Or, is it
because the Indian Treaties involved here are slightly more
than one hundred? Or is it because the non-Indian population
has increased in that century in this area from 3,900 to more
than 3,000,000?

Citizenship for the Indian has too frequently been used as
a convenience of government for deprivation of rights and
property held owing to our being Indians. We did not generally become citizens of this Nation nor lawful residents of
its States until June 2, 1924—and not when all other people
gained nationality and citizenship under the Fourteenth
Amendment in 1868, the "due process" and "equal protection
of law" amendment. Indians did not become citizens under
this Act since it was immediately held in the U.S. Supreme
Court that Indians were born unto the allegiance of their
Tribes and not unto the allegiance of the United States. The
granting of citizenship was not to act negatively upon Indian
allegiance nor rights.

It is such first Allegiance that I now declare and embrace
in making total commitment to the Indian Cause and the
immediate fight for undiminished Fishing Rights.

There is no reason why Indian people should not be permitted to fish in the waters where these rights exist. There
is no reason why Indians should spend their lives in the
courts, in jail, or under the dominion of fear. There is no
legitimate reason why this Nation and the State of Washington can not respect the equitable interests and rights of
Indian people and be responsive to our needs.

The oldest skeletal human remains ever found in the Western Hemisphere were recently uncovered on the banks of the Columbia River—the remains of Indian fishermen. What kind of government or society would spend millions of dollars to pick upon our bones, restore our ancestral life patterns, and protect our ancient remains from damage—while at the same time eating upon the flesh of our living people with power processes that hate our existence as Indians, and which would now destroy us and the way of life we now choose—and by all rights are entitled to live?

We will fight for these Rights and we will live our life!

IS THE TREND CHANGING?

by Laura McCloud

Among some of the Indians of western Washington State the true meaning of the fight for their fishing rights was epitomized by the name they gave to an organization that they formed to give solidity to their struggle — The Survival of American Indians Association, Inc. One of its first members was Janet McCloud, a Tulalip Indian who was married to a Puyallup Indian and was the mother of eight children.

From the beginning she and her husband were leaders in the fishing rights struggle. On October 13, 1965, they were among six Indians arrested and jailed for fishing at their usual fishing site at Frank's Landing on Washington's Nisqually River. Their trial was not held until January 15, 1969. By then Mrs. McCloud had become an embattled champion for Indian rights and was known to Indians throughout the country for her courage and devotion to traditional Indian values. Many Indians, as well as non-Indians, who knew and admired her, were interested in the outcome of the January 15 trial. The following report, written by Laura McCloud, one of her daughters, and circulated among the defendants' well-wishers, provides an intimate glimpse of an experience that has become almost routine to Indians fighting for their survival.

On October 13, 1965, we held a "fish-in" on the Nisqually River to try and bring a focus on our fishing fight with the State of Washington. The "fish-in" started at 4:00 p.m. and was over at about 4:30 p.m. It ended with 6 Indians in jail and dazed Indian kids wondering "what happened?"

My parents, Don & Janet McCloud; Al and Maiselle Bridges; Suzan Satiacum and Don George Jr. were arrested that day. They were released after posting bail a few hours later. The charges against these six Indians was "obstructing the duty of a police officer." Now all we could do was wait till the trials started. There was a seventh Indian who was later arrested for the same charge, Nugent Kautz. And he had not been at Frank's Landing on that day.

The trial was to begin on January 15, 1969, at 9:30 a.m. We went into the courthouse that Wednesday certain that we would not receive justice as was proven to us in other trials. As we walked into the hallways there were many game wardens standing there, some dressed in their uniforms and some in plain clothes, but we recognized all of them.

Many of us were dressed in our traditional way with headbands, leggings and necklaces. As we walked the length of the corridor to the courtroom, the game wardens were looking us up and down, laughing at us. I said to my cousin, "Don't pay any attention to them, they don't know any better." The three leaders of this "gestapo" group were present in the corridor, "Colonel Custer" Neubrech, and his henchmen Buzz Sawyer from the game department and Zimmerman, field marshal. We kind of had to laugh at these men because they were strutting around like roosters. Any person, even if they did not realize what was going on, but sensitive to feeling could probably feel the bad vibrations emanating from one side of the hallway to the other side. The tension was very high at all times. There were many Indians present at the trial, some from very far away. And as usual one Indian was arrested. In every trial I have attended they usually arrest some Indian.

The trial began a few minutes off schedule. The Deputy Prosecuting Attorney was a new man, his name was Judd—he acted very cocky and over confident. Judd's director was the State game and Fisheries department legal advisor, Mike Johnson. Our attorney was Al Ziontz, an American Civil Liberties Union volunteer.

The first witness for the State was a field marshal for the game department—Zimmerman. He stated that he was directing the game wardens at the Landing on Oct. 13. He was in charge of the reinforcements from all over the State that came down on us like a sea of green. At the time of the fish-in I thought that there were about a hundred game wardens.

The next State witness was the public relations-man for the game department. He had 16 millimeter motion pictures to show. He had been posing as a newsman on the day of the fish-in. Our attorney objected to the pictures because they could have been cut and fixed to the State's advantage or taken for the State's advantage. But the State got their way and the motion pictures were shown. And to this moment I can not understand why they wanted these pictures shown because they sure looked better for our side than for theirs.

The parade of State witnesses were all either game wardens or fisheries patrolmen. All these men swore oaths to their God to tell the truth. It is my opinion that it seemed to them just a farce because everyone of them lied under oath. They were all asked if any of them carried weapons or if they had seen any wardens carrying weapons. Doughtery a game warden was the last State witness. He had the audacity to state that a fish could be caught in a net with no lead line or weights to hold it down. A net consists of three main parts; a lead line on the bottom to hold it down, the main part is the middle which is the nylon mesh, and on top of the net a cork line to hold the net up. Now, without a leadline the net will just float on the top of the water. All I can say is, "Boy, these guys teach us new things all the time." The idea of catching a fish in a net without a leadline is absolutely absurd —the game wardens must think the fish are trying to get caught. Yeah, they just jump up into the net.

After these gamewardens went on the stand the prosecutor attorney said they had one more witness but he could not be there until the next day. So the judge said the trial would be adjourned until 9:30 the next morning.

The trial started late again the next morning (1/16/69). The State started off with their last witness, State Fisheries Biologist, Lasseter. He talked about how we Indians are the ones who depleted the fish in the Puyallup River and if we weren't controlled we would do the same to the Nisqually River. The Puyallup River is filled with pollution more than it is with water. And why would we want to wipe out our livelihood? Our attorney made Lasseter state that it could have been the pollution not the Indians who depleted the fish in the Puyallup River.

Now, it was our turn! The first witness for our defense was Bob Johnson. At the time of the fish-in he was the editor of the "Auburn Citizen" newspaper. He told of the tactics the game wardens used on us. Mr. Johnson also had evidence with him, pictures of the game wardens, showing billie clubs and seven celled flashlights. The Prosecuting attorney got real shook up about these. It seemed like he was saying "I object" every few minutes.

The next witness was a Mrs. Flanigan, a psychologist who had been with Bob Johnson, to be an impartial witness. She said she thought that this fish-in would be boring because of the other one she had attended at Brando's Landing at the Puyallup River. But after this incident she became a believer and had led her to help start an organization to help the Indian people.

The next defense witness was Janet McCloud, Tulalip Indian. She told the facts about why the Indians had had the fish-in demonstration on that day and what the mood the Indians had before the fish-in. This was important because the State thought we were after blood that day. And we were not expecting any violence because all my brothers and sisters were there and the youngest was 4 at that time. And if we had expected any violence none of the children would have been there. She told how she felt when she realized that the game wardens were going to ram our boat and how she felt when she realized these men meant business with their 7-celled flashlights, billie clubs, and brass knuckles. My two little brothers were in that boat when it was rammed, the youngest was 7 and could not swim. Besides, once you get tangled in nylon mesh it is very easy to drown. While she was telling this story, we could tell she was trying very hard to keep from crying, but this did not help because she started to. And every Indian in that courtroom that was there that horrible day started to remember the fear and anger that they had felt that day. The fear was not for one's self but for each other. We had the fear the Indians at SAND CREEK must have felt

—and we started to remember more vividly. It took all the strength we had to keep from crying too! We did not want these men to see us weak again.

The trial stopped for a few minutes while the Deputy prosecuting attorney went out to get a drink of water for Janet McCloud. He returned with it and handed it to Janet and just as she started to take a drink, Craig Carpenter jumped up and said, "Janet don't drink that water. You don't know what he put in it!" Indians knowing our history know what has happened to many leaders in the past by the State. Craig was asked to leave the courtroom. And he had come up all the way from California to be at this trial.

The next witness was Don McCloud, Puyallup Indian. He was one of the Indian men in the boat that day. He told how the boat was rammed. (Oh, incidentally, the game wardens said that they did not ram the boat.) He also said how he had seen a game warden with a steel pipe and how a game warden tried to knee him in the groin. And the other acts of violence that he had witnessed the game wardens doing.

The next witness was Nugent Kautz, a Puyallup Indian. He told how he had not been present at the fish-in but was in school at Tacoma.

With all this testimony and evidence, it was plain to see that the game wardens had lied. We only hoped that the jury would believe our side of the fish-in story. We also learned the names of the game wardens whose pictures we had, especially the one who had been beating on Alison and Valerie Bridges.

Mr. Ziontz called one last witness—a hostile one—a game warden. This was the one who had been carrying a leather slapper which the Indians confiscated on 1/13/65 from his hip-pocket and had entered as evidence. His name was engraved on the slapper. He admitted that it was his and had been taken out his pocket but he said that he never used it.

The State called "Colonel Custer" Neubrech for their rebuttal witness. He said at the briefing he had given his men the night before the fish-in he had told them to have extreme patience with the Indians. Either they don't know the meaning of extreme patience or else they didn't understand him right. Whatever, they didn't have this patience.

After the two lawyers gave their summations the jury went into session. This was at ten o'clock at night. They were out until midnight. The foreman came in first and said, "The rest are afraid to come in." I thought, here comes another guilty. When the foreman handed the judge the decision the room became very silent. Then the judge read, "The jury finds the defendant Nugent Kautz 'not guilty.' " He read the rest of the names with the same verdict. I didn't believe it. I turned to my cousin and said, "Did I hear right?" She nodded her head, yes. Everyone was happy, except for the State. The game wardens were very hostile after this.

Footnote: The game wardens, incensed at the adverse verdict, left the Tyee Motel where they had been celebrating, prematurely, their victory and went down in large numbers to Frank's Landing. A sympathetic soul overheard the wardens and called the Landing to warn the Indians. Nevertheless the wardens caught a car load of Indians at the railroad trestle and surrounded them in their state game cars—they proceeded to hit the Indians' car with their nightsticks, cussing them and trying to provoke Al Bridges and Hank Adams to fight. It was obvious to the Indians that they had been drinking. This took place about 2 a.m. The next day two Indian boys were walking to the store when a carload of game wardens stopped them and Walter Neubrech, chief enforcement officer, game dept., asked Russell McCloud why the Indians didn't have any nets in the river last night. He told him that he did not know. Neubrech went on to say that he had given his men orders to use their clubs on any Indian who goes fishing and to use them freely. So the war goes on—which goes to prove that the history books are wrong when they talk about "the last Indian wars." They have never stopped! Janet McCloud.

THE AMERICAN INDIAN AND THE BUREAU OF INDIAN AFFAIRS

A Study, with Recommendations
by Alvin M. Josephy, Jr.
February 11, 1969

When the Democrats left office in 1969, the record of the preceding eight years showed a steadily intensifying Indian demand for self-determination, beginning with the Chicago "Declaration of Indian Purpose" of 1961 and coming from more and more elements of the Indian population. Save for some lip service, however, and a slight groping in the direction of permitting Indians to have a greater participatory role in discussing and managing programs that were framed in Washington for them, the eight-year record also showed that both the Kennedy and Johnson administrations had remained, on the whole, indifferent to the trend that had been taking place among the Indians. The one bright spot, for a time at least, had been the OEO antipoverty programs, but they were special. No important change had occurred in either policy or substance in the more vital relationship between the Bureau of Indian Affairs and the Indians, and an observer could conclude that the Democrats for eight years had continued the governmental attitudes about Indians that they had inherited from the past: the assimilation of the Indians was still the ultimate national goal, and the Indians were still judged not competent enough to know what was best for them.

In actuality, this is what had occurred in the 1961–69 period. The real rulers of Indian policy were not in the Department of the Interior, but in the congressional committees on Interior and Insular Affairs and in the Bureau of the Budget. Both held a whip hand over the Secretary of the Interior and his Bureau of Indian Affairs in regard to direction, thrust, and appropriations for Indian policies and programs, and both had clung stubbornly to the non-Indians' traditional ideas of what was best for the Indians. By 1969 both were still deaf to the Indians' rising demand for control of their own affairs, and both had the power to prevent any meaningful response by the Department of the

Interior to what the Indians wanted. The result, in effect, was that the Bureau of Indian Affairs, the agency of government responsible for the Indians' welfare, was accountable not to the Indians whom it was supposed to serve and protect, but to powerful bodies hostile to Indian self-determination, the congressional committees and the Bureau of the Budget.

Nevertheless the Indians, remembering with bitterness that termination of federal relations with the tribes had been the policy of the Eisenhower regime, the last Republican administration in office, faced the prospect of the Nixon administration with considerable uncertainty, and even fear. On September 27, 1968, during his campaign for election, Nixon had promised the Indians that termination of tribal recognition would not be "a policy objective" of his administration and that in no case would termination be imposed without their consent. The Indians had applauded that statement, but after the election they looked for a more concrete assertion from the President-elect, guaranteeing that the September promise had not been campaign oratory and spelling out for them in specific terms what the new administration's Indian policy would be.

The position of the Indians in American society, in truth, had reached a point where decisive change could occur. In the view of many, the time for the realization of self-determination had arrived. A new administration, willing to assume the initiative in bringing new attitudes to Congress and the Bureau of the Budget, could respond to the Indians' demands for control and power over their own affairs while continuing to observe treaty obligations and protect the Indians' lands and resources.

On the eve of assuming office, the new administration recognized that at the very least it would have to make a clean break with the termination image it had inherited from the Republicans of the 1950's. But it was out of touch with the Indians of 1969. It took President Nixon many months to find an Indian Commissioner of Indian Affairs acceptable to the Republican party. It took him a year and a half to frame and announce his administration's Indian policy. In the meantime, Republican officials conscientiously acquainted themselves with the Indians and their needs.

The following document was one of the first foundations upon which the new administration developed the Indian policy that it eventually proclaimed in July, 1970. The document was written in January and February, 1969, at the request of the President-elect and served as a briefing for him on the then-current status of Indian affairs and on events in federal-Indian relations during the Democratic administrations of the 1960's. Such a background, providing orientation as well as recommendations based on the Indians' own expressed desires and proposals for solutions to their needs, was considered necessary before the new administration could proceed to consider its own policy.

The first section of the report, taking note of the Indians' continued opposition to the termination policy and of their fears that the new Republican administration would revive it, recommends that the President re-enunciate his promise on termination given the Indians in September, 1968. This was ultimately done, first by Vice President Spiro Agnew and Secretary of the Interior Walter Hickel to the National Congress of American Indians in October, 1969, and finally by the President in his Message to Congress on Indian Affairs in July, 1970.

The report's second section, titled "The Context of This Study," is basically an orientation lesson in history and points of view for non-Indians dealing with federal-Indian relations in 1969. The third section is a chronological recapitulation of studies and major developments in Indian affairs during the 1961–1969 period, revealing the steady Indian demand for self-determination and the government's continued deafness to it. It concludes with the admonition that the time has come to make Indian self-determination a reality, but points out that certain governmental obstacles stand in the way. One of those obstacles, the responsibility of the Department of the Interior to interests that competed with the Indians, is dealt with in the fourth section, which proposes transferring the Bureau of Indian Affairs to the Executive Office of the President, but suggests, also, several alternative solutions. The second obstacle, deficiencies in the structure of the Bureau of Indian Affairs that worked inherently to prevent Indian self-determination from becoming a reality, is examined in the fifth section, which also suggests how the bureau might be reorganized. The report's final section discusses specific Indian programs and recommends that they be initiated, planned, and carried out under Indian control and direction.

Following are excerpts from the various sections of the report.

I. A FIRST PRIORITY

It is the purpose of this study to provide an understanding of the shape and substance of present-day federal-Indian relationships and the ability of the Bureau of Indian Affairs to serve efficiently as a vehicle for the management of those relations, as well as to make recommendations for a course upon which to embark in 1969. But among the questions to be examined are where, if not in the Interior Department, functions of federal-Indian relationships should be placed; what, if any, restructuring should be considered within the Bureau of Indian Affairs; which programs and their administration require changes? Any proposed alteration from the status quo would obviously stir again the embers of the Indians' fear of termination. . . .

Therefore this study is preceded by an initial proposal, the purpose of which is to remove as effectively as possible the fear of termination as a motive from the body of the study itself and the recommendations it includes.

It is not necessary to argue the wrongs versus the motives of the termination period of 1953–58, or review the specifics of the human damage that occurred. Recognition that the policy should not again be enforced is today so widespread that Indians, as well as all non-Indians knowledgeable about Indian affairs, enthusiastically applauded the statement by President Nixon, addressed to the Indian people through the National Congress of American Indians, on September 27, 1968, during his campaign for election: "Termination of tribal recognition will not be a policy objective, and in no case will it be imposed without Indian consent."

This was a clear, reassuring statement, but now that the new administration has assumed office it requires, at the earliest convenient opportunity, reiteration to the Indian tribes and peoples. There is a new Secretary of the Interior. It is obvious that there is a new look being taken at Indian affairs. The Indians are again nervous. During the next to last week of January, 1969, the Executive Committee of the National Congress of American Indians met in Washington. The Republicans, under whom the termination policy had been enforced, were back in power. Was a campaign promise to be kept? What was really going to happen? The Indians could not find out and went home uneasily. Their distress, already communicated to numerous non-Indian groups interested in their progress, is heightened by the realization of the unique relationship of the Indians to the American government, resting, as it does, on the sober fact that Congress has plenary power over the tribes. Unlike all other Americans, the Indians are subject to policies that have been made for them, often against their will. They are peculiarly sensitive to every nuance of government, for that government, they believe, can do anything it wishes with their lives, property and fortunes. Hence, the administration and its Indian policies is their all, frightfully close to them, frightfully meaningful.

It is therefore recommended that the Administration, hopefully through the President himself, find and take advantage of an opportunity to address the Indian people, possibly through the National Congress of American Indians in Washington, re-enunciating the statement given the Indians on September 27, 1968, particularly as it refers to termination, and making clear that the new Administration has no intention of disrupting the Indian peoples by new directions in policy, but will carry out the promises made on September 27, 1968, and make them meaningful.

Such a statement will not only have great meaning for the American Indians and prepare the ground for productive federal-Indian relations in the years immediately ahead, but will receive the approving reaction of all alienated and dispossessed peoples as well as those in the United States and in other nations to whom the treatment of the American Indians is symbolic of the broadest attitudes of the Administration.

II. THE CONTEXT OF THIS STUDY

It has been said often enough, and with great truth, that expert knowledge of the cultures and histories, not alone of Indians generally, but of the many separate tribes, is needed to understand Indian needs, desires, actions, and responses, as well as to work intelligently and compassionately with Indians to help frame, administer, and service policies and programs for their benefit.

There is no doubt that many of the failures and frustrations that mark the course of federal-Indian relations, past and present, can be ascribed to deficiencies of knowledge about Indians among non-Indians who are involved in managing Indian affairs. Indians have long complained about officials who listen to them but don't seem to understand them, and many of the complaints and criticisms that Indians level at the Bureau of Indian Affairs result from actions and programs that were imposed by well-intentioned whites, but bear no relation to the realities of what a tribe, fashioned by a particular history and culture, needed, desired or could accept and carry out with success.

The Peace Corps, which oriented its enrollees in the backgrounds and cultures of the peoples to whom they were being sent, might have taught the Bureau of Indian Affairs a lesson. But even today, little attention is paid to such instruction of Bureau personnel, and in its proper place in this study a recommendation will be made on that subject. In this section, however, it is appropriate to make several general observations as necessary prerequisites for a more vivid understanding of the implications of the findings and recommendations in the following portions of this study. In a sense they provide a basis and context for a realistic approach to federal-Indian relations in 1969 and to what, if anything, requires rethinking and change.

1) In the great mass of treaties, statutes, laws and regulations that have been built up during the long course of federal-Indian relations, the non-Indian, to use an analogy, often becomes lost among the trees of Indian affairs and too rarely steps back far enough to see the forest whole. He forgets basic truths about Indians that must never be forgotten, if only because they are in the minds of the Indians with whom non-Indians are trying to work. It would appear unnecessary to restate such facts that the Indians were here for thousands of years; that this is their homeland; that they evolved their own distinctive cultures and did not share the points of view, attitudes, and thinking that came to the rest of the American population from Judeo-Christian and Western Civilization legacies; that although the Indians were conquered militarily (and are the only portion of the American population that reflects that experience), they are confirming a lesson of history, namely that no people has ever been coerced by another people into scuttling its own culture; and that although acculturation and assimilation do occur, they occur only on the individual's own terms. The awareness of such generalizations makes clear the implications of a further facet of Indian affairs that has continuing relevancy, and especially to this study, namely the Indians' position, and therefore their posture, vis-a-vis the government.

In matters that are of the most importance to them, the

Indians, unlike all other Americans, do not yet enjoy self-government. They are still governed, not entirely unlike colonial subjects, by strangers whom they neither elected nor appointed and who are not accountable to them. As late as 1934 the rule of the "governor" was absolute; since then, tribal councils, like the legislatures of many modern colonies, have acquired authority over a broadening range of tribal affairs. But the "governor" is still present with the apparatus of management and the powers of direction, influence, finances and veto to use when and where they really count. The practical meaning of this relationship of the American government to its Indian citizens in this extraordinarily late day and age was noted recently in a study titled "The Indian: The Forgotten American," published in the *Harvard Law Review* in June, 1968. Its authors, Warren H. Cohen and Philip J. Mause, commented: "The BIA possesses final authority over most tribal actions as well as over many decisions made by Indians as individuals. BIA approval is required, for example, when a tribe enters into a contract, expends money, or amends its constitution. Although normal expectation in American society is that a private individual or group may do anything unless it is specifically prohibited by the government, it might be said that the normal expectation on the reservation is that the Indians may not do anything unless it is specifically permitted by the government."

The psychological implications of the Indians' status as compared with that of the rest of the American body politic loom with increasing significance in Indian affairs today, especially as larger numbers of young Indians become educated and motivated to seek the full measure of self-government enjoyed by all other Americans. To an extent, the full perspective of this "forest-view" of all Indians is obscured by dilemmas posed by the obligatory trust function of the government. But a banker, exercising a trust function for a non-Indian citizen, applies himself only to the substance of the trust and does not govern the life of his client or necessarily manage his other affairs. One task in Indian affairs is inevitably to narrow the trustee's domain to the substance of the trust (to be discussed later) and to remove his authority from other areas. The logic of attempting to achieve such a goal can, again, only be appreciated in full by viewing the "forest" whole, and not being enmeshed and inhibited among the trees.

2) To the incoming member of a new Administration the questions and problems of federal-Indian relations are of the here and now. Decisions concerning changes or the retention of the status quo will be made largely within the context of today alone. But to the Indian, the context is an immensely broader one and possesses a vividness and influence that often leads to the frustration and failure of policies and programs when the non-Indian administrator fails to comprehend its relevancy. The context is history, the details and individual steps of which may be unknown to the contemporary non-Indian official, but are still intimate and potent in Indian thinking and responses.

To the Indian, 1969 is a continuation of an unbroken narrative of policies, programs and promises, often abruptly changing, disorganizing, contradictory, and unrealistic, and of people, many of them still personally remembered, who gave promises and orders and who sometimes worked for good and sometimes for harm. In Washington discussions will occur today, and policies and programs will be considered according to the current situation. But the Indian's mind will also be on a legacy of pacification, army and missionary rule, punishments and repression, allotments, treaty sessions and sacred promises, laws and special rights acknowledged in return for land cessions, and orders given by the government in the 1920's, countermanded in the 1930's, countermanded again in the 1950's, and countermanded once more in the 1960's. Specifically, the Indian's response will be conditioned by the knowledge of a Mr. Smith or a Captain Jones who came to the reservation as the agent of a President in the mid-nineteenth century and told the tribal leaders something that their descendants have kept alive from generation to generation. He will color his reactions to a proposal with the evergreen memories of battles won or lost, of injuries and injustices, of land taken from his people by fraud, deceit and corruption, of lost hunting, fishing and water rights, and of zigzag policies of administrations that came to office, just like the new one, and then left.

The full range of these influences cannot always be known or appreciated by the non-Indian, but a maximum awareness of their existence and nature will inevitably contribute to the attainment of greater realism and higher hopes of success in the conduct of Indian affairs. For the immediate future, as one example, disorientations caused by dizzying alterations in Indian policy from one administration to the next in the past warns against sharp new changes, or hints of such changes, in fundamental policies today.

3) Despite the fear of termination and various programmatic and administrative shortcomings, some of which were quite serious and will be discussed in later sections, a number of profound and important improvements did occur in Indian affairs during the last eight years. One of them, fraught with significance for the future direction of Indian affairs, requires the most serious recognition.

Indians had long asserted, but usually to deaf ears, that the individual tribes knew better than the government what kinds of programs they needed and wanted, and that if they could play decisive roles in the planning of such programs, they could, with technical and financial assistance, demonstrate an ability to learn quickly to administer and execute them successfully.

This assertion was stated forcibly in a "Declaration of Indian Purpose" by some 420 Indian leaders of 67 tribes at a gathering in Chicago in June, 1961, but, although endorsed to some extent by Secretary Udall's Task Force the same year, received no serious recognition or encouragement from the Bureau of Indian Affairs. The Indians were deemed not to know what was best for them, and programs continued to be imposed on them.

During the first years of the operations of programs of the Office of Economic Opportunity on reservations, however, what is now considered a momentous breakthrough finally did occur. Under the OEO's initial approach, based on "maximum feasible participation" by the recipients of the programs in shaping and guiding them, tribes were asked by the new agency to frame aid programs for themselves, and when they were approved and funded, the Indians for the first time on a significant scale managed the programs and the monies allocated to them. Many of the programs were executed successfully, and numerous Indians for the first time gained confidence as well as experience in administration and management. Most importantly, Indian initiative had been mobilized and encouraged, and the new self-assurance was soon reflected in increased demands by the Indians to the Bureau of Indian Affairs and other agencies of government that the tribes be allowed to play decisive roles in determining their own needs and developing their own programs. During the last few years the BIA and other agencies have begun to respond in a cautious and tentative manner. But negativism, outmoded regulations and crippling features of certain acts still impede the full freeing of Indian initiative and energies, and defects in the internal structure of the BIA preclude a meaningful development of Indian self-management. One of the first considerations of the new Administration, it would appear, is to determine not whether to accede to the historical development among the Indians, but how to do it—a matter that will receive attention in a later section of this study.

4) In the same vein, it must be noted that the non-Indian population of the United States, reacting to a multitude of winds of change abroad in the world in recent years, is beginning to turn away from a long-held view regarding the Indian's destiny—and therefore from what were long considered the proper policies and programs for him. From the time of Jamestown and Plymouth, the most benign attitude of the white man concerning Indians was, assimilate or die. Missionaries and agencies of government tried to rush Indians into becoming Christianized farmers, and from the administration of George Washington until the present day national policy, stated or implicit, has been directed toward the turning of the Indian into a white man, the alternative seeming to be

only continued primitivism, economic stagnation, and ultimate obliteration by white society. All programs, actions and attitudes of government have supported this policy which derived its mandate from the non-Indian population and its representatives in Congress.

At the same time, a minority opinion always existed that expressed the view that Indian progress and development, far from being assisted, was actually being crippled and delayed by the "either-or" choice, that Indians would resist attempts to force and hurry their assimilation, and that such attempts would not only fail to achieve their purpose but were morally wrong, since no people had the right to strip a culture from another people. Inevitably, the merits of the point of view of the latter group were obscured by superficial and erroneous arguments that they were more interested in seeing Indian cultures preserved than allowing the Indians to develop, and the minority was unable to bring about a meaningful dialogue that might have produced an impact on national policy, which throughout the Kennedy and Johnson administrations continued, in essence, to point toward the ultimate goal of Indian assimilation.

Of late, however, Indian articulateness, studies of Indian education, and changing attitudes among the American people concerning minority groups have combined to pose the acceptance of a different destiny for the American Indians, one in which they would be allowed to develop on their own terms and at their own chosen rate of speed — bi-culturally if they so desired — being assisted to create a viable economic life for their people, but not being pressured to give up any parts of their individual cultures which they wished to retain, and not being urged to take on any of the dominant society's traits which they did not want. The pros and cons of such a policy need not be argued here. But the strength, particularly among the Indians, of those who maintain that Indian self-determination is now the surest road to Indian progress and development, that it will see a new and electrifying rebirth of Indian initiative and vigor, and that its result will be the growth of viable and healthy Indian communities within the nation, has grown to the point where the new administration must take note of the areas in which it may soon engender significant confrontations.

The regions of highest sensitivity, perhaps, where appreciation for Indian self-determination has met its greatest resistance in the past are the Bureau of the Budget, the Solicitor's Office of the Department of the Interior, and the Senate Committee on Interior and Insular Affairs. Commitment by key persons in those areas to the traditional policy of assimilation-or-continued stagnation has had an enormous influence in shaping Indian programs, for better or worse, and in defining the thrust and direction of the Bureau of Indian Affairs' conduct of Indian relations. If there is to be a change in governmental attitudes regarding the justice and potential for progress inherent in the acceptance of the Indians' right of self-determination, it will only come about because the Bureau of the Budget and the Congress have been persuaded that the traditional approach has been proved to be self-defeating. In the meantime, those areas will be expected to interpose effective blocks to measures that bear the appearance of slowing the process of assimilation, whatever their other intent may be. (One recent example may be offered: In his Message to Congress on American Indian Affairs on March 6, 1968, President Johnson announced that he was directing the Secretary of the Interior to establish and train Indian parent school boards for federal Indian schools. Despite the fact that this was a response to a considerable body of opinion among Indians as well as non-Indian educators, and had been recommended by a special Interagency Task Force of the federal government, it is understood that the Bureau of the Budget questioned certain ramifications of the proposal and has to date inhibited the Bureau of Indian Affairs from effectively implementing the Presidential directive.)

Within the Bureau of Indian Affairs there are disciples of both policies and a dichotomy that cannot and will not endure indefinitely without producing internal conflicts in the Bureau apparatus and confusion among the Indians. The Bureau adheres officially to the traditional assimilationist point of view, but even the present Commissioner pays lip service to the Indian self-determinists, though he can do little to make it meaningful on the reservations. Some of the more forceful Bureau members in the field who would like to adapt programs and approaches to the Indians' demands for self-determination try to find small ways in which they can chip away at the old policy. The others believe genuinely in the traditional policy or try dutifully to smother their beliefs or live with frustrations about which they can do nothing.

The Indians' demand for self-determination will increase steadily, but there will be many ways to move soundly with it. Perhaps the best way, short of the enunciation of an Administration point of view on the subject, will be a clear and purposeful redefinement of the Bureau of Indian Affairs' functions, procedures and limits of authority, together with a restructuring of the Bureau to accommodate to the changes. Though the changes would not be drastic, intentions and effects on the reservations would be altered, and a natural process tending toward increased self-determination would come into play. Any such change from the status quo would, of course, require the support of the Congress and the Bureau of the Budget and would demand that the Administration play a positive persuasive role with both bodies. . . .

III. STUDIES AND MAJOR DEVELOPMENTS IN
THE LAST EIGHT YEARS

"During the last eight years," an Indian leader said recently, "Indian policies and programs have been studied to death. What we need is for someone to begin paying attention to some of the things that the Indians recommended in those studies."

The record provides reasonable grounds for such a complaint. The period 1961–68 saw a series of studies made, both within and outside the government, on Indian affairs. Each of them produced numerous policy, program and administrative recommendations, many of which were afterward adopted and implemented. But from the Indian point of view, some of the most significant recommendations, especially those which had come from the Indians themselves, were never carried out because a) their implications for the Indian people were not understood; or b) they required abrupt changes in attitudes toward Indians which the government was unwilling to make; or c) the studies were deficient in that they endorsed the recommendations in principle but failed to come to grips with the question of whether the Bureau of Indian Affairs, as constituted and directed, could (or would) execute the programs effectively.

The need of the present Administration to know and judge the current status and character of federal-Indian relations is an echo of a need similarly felt, to a greater or lesser degree, by each previous incoming administration. Eight years ago, when the Kennedy Administration entered office with a burst of vigor and a spate of fresh ideas, characterized by such "New Frontier" concepts as the Peace Corps and the Alliance for Progress, it conveyed to the American Indians its intention that they, too, would be the recipients of new and dynamic thinking and action that would strive to solve problems that had long defied solution. But the first job was to conduct a thorough study of the status of Indian affairs, and for this Secretary of the Interior Udall . . . appointed a Task Force, consisting of its chairman, W. W. Keeler, an executive of the Phillips Petroleum Company and Principal Chief of the Cherokee Nation of Oklahoma; Philleo Nash, an anthropologist and former assistant to President Truman and Lieutenant Governor of Wisconsin who was to become Commissioner of Indian Affairs; William Zimmerman, a former Acting Commissioner of Indian Affairs; and James E. Officer, an anthropologist at the University of Arizona who had come to Washington to assist Secretary Udall. In a preliminary meeting on February 9, 1961, with members of the Task Force and various officials of the Interior Department, Udall stated that his goal was "an administrative reorganization and policy reorganization of the Indian Bureau."

The Task Force held hearings among Indian groups throughout the country, studied the Bureau, conferred with numerous Indian interest organizations, religious groups, members of Congressional committees and their staffs, the Bureau of the Budget, tribal attorneys, private groups and individuals, members of bureaus within the Department of the Interior and other government agencies, and on July 10, 1961, submitted its report, with recommendations, to the Secretary. By then the momentum of the new administration had slowed, the Bureau of Indian Affairs had been proceeding for six months under the new administration, and the report, which was neither as fresh nor as hard-hitting as the Indians had hoped it would be, was something of an anti-climax. In September, 1961, Philleo Nash was appointed Commissioner, replacing the Acting Commissioner, John O. Crow, and under Nash the Bureau adjusted gradually to a slow and piecemeal implementation of some of the Task Force's recommendations.

There is no need in 1969 to repeat the experience of the Kennedy Administration of 1961 with another full-fledged, Task Force-type study of Indian affairs, complete with months of hearings and subordinate studies. . . .

A brief conclusion from the . . . record of what has, and has not, occurred during the last eight years illuminates the following:

1) Both the appropriations and functions of the Bureau of Indian Affairs have increased greatly, and many other Federal agencies, including the OEO, EDA, HAA, the Office of Education, and the Labor Department, now share the reservation scene with the BIA;

2) The BIA's greatest expansion has occurred in the fields of education, vocational training and placement, housing, and industrial and community development, and is evidence that a change in its orientation from the primacy of its trust function to that of development has become an established fact;

3) The obligations conferred by the trust function still require the wielding of authority over other matters by Bureau officials and result in many of the conflicts between the Bureau and the Indians, as well as much of the BIA's negativism and delays. Increasingly, the Indians are re-

questing the right to assume full responsibility for the management of their income and final authority over such matters as attorney contracts, tribal codes, and constitutional actions — while having their lands continue inviolate in trust status;

4) The principle of self-determination has been accepted and is already being applied in small ways on some reservations. The BIA has begun a trend of negotiating with tribes to permit them, through contracts, to provide some services; this too is encouraging the process of self-determination. But Indian participation and decision-making are still the exception and are being frustrated and denied too regularly by the Bureau's present organization;

5) At the same time, the BIA's structure still leads to a malaise within the Bureau as bad as eight years ago that positively holds back progress;

6) *The top priority is for a change in the administration of Indian affairs to accelerate Indian progress and achieve the maximum effective implementation of Indian polices and programs by utilizing, and not impeding, the Indians' development of self-determination.*

IV. POSITIONING INDIAN AFFAIRS IN
THE FEDERAL GOVERNMENT

This study now addresses itself to specific recommendations for a course upon which to embark in 1969, including:

The positioning of the administration of Indian affairs within the government;

The reorganization of the BIA's structure;

Programmatic approaches.

This section concerns the first of those items.

Much thought, time and energy has been expended in the past in trying to determine where best to place the administration of Indian affairs within the Executive branch of the government. The Fund for the Republic Report in 1961 examined proposals "to improve the administration of Indian affairs" that included abolishing the BIA entirely, with no substitute; transferring it entirely to HEW; spreading its functions among other Federal Departments and Bureaus (law and order to Justice, forestry to Agriculture, etc.); creating an independent Indian Authority like TVA; or transferring responsibility to the States (termination). It decided that the best answer was to keep the BIA where it was in Interior, with the Bureau "assuming somewhat altered responsibilities and functions. The Bureau has the decided advantage of being already in the field," the Report added. "It needs only revision and redirection to accomplish the purposes which the present-day situation of the Indian demands." (The Bureau stayed in Interior, but . . . it was not revised or redirected.)

In 1966 an HEW–Interior Interdepartmental Committee turned down a proposal to transfer the BIA's educational function to HEW. . . . The BIA's health function had been transferred to the Public Health Service in HEW in 1955, but the circumstances were different. The Public Health Service had an established, operating and highly professional apparatus that could accommodate itself to enfolding a Division of Indian Health; there was no established school structure or experience in operating a school system in HEW's Office of Education.

Nevertheless, in 1966, too, the Presidential Task Force . . . made a strong proposal to transfer Indian affairs in toto from the Interior Department, whose programs emphasized conservation and natural resources, to Health, Education and Welfare, whose programs were concerned essentially with human development. The functions of the BIA were not to be scattered among the various branches of HEW, but were to "be transferred to a single new agency" in that Department, with a "direct reporting channel to the Secretary, probably through an Administrator for Indian Affairs." An important point, not articulated by the Task Force's Report, but obvious to many of its readers, including the leadership of the House Interior and Insular Affairs Committee, whose opposition to the proposed transfer went far to bury the entire Report, was that the separation of the Indians from the Interior Department implied, as well, the transfer of Indian affairs to other Committees in Congress and to other sections of the Bureau of the Budget. This may, indeed, have been a motive of the Task Force, for the Interior Committees of Congress and the Interior section of the Bureau of the Budget, no less than the Department of the Interior, are also oriented primarily toward natural resources, rather than human development.

Following the shelving of the Presidential Task Force's Report, the Interagency Task Force recommended keeping the Bureau of Indian Affairs in the Department of the Interior, but placing it under a new "people-oriented" Assistant Secretary of the Interior for Indian and Territorial Affairs. This was not accepted by the White House, and in January, 1969, Indian leadership, through the National Congress of American Indians, proposed to the new Administration the establishment of the Bureau as an independent commission or agency.

The primary urgency in Indian affairs facing the new Administration in 1969 is the reorganization of the present Bureau of Indian Affairs. . . . How to accomplish that most smoothly and effectively to assist the Indians must determine where the administration of Indian affairs is to be positioned.

This study recommends that a meaningful and determined reorganization of the administration of Indian affairs, together with the providing of an effective Administration thrust to go forward to the opportunities of tomorrow and not simply solve the problems of yesterday, can only be accomplished by moving the Bureau of Indian Affairs to the Executive Office of the Presidency, for the objectives of Indian affairs in 1969 require nothing less than the priority, mandate and visibility which the President himself can give them. . . .

The principal argument for this recommended move is stated in the proposal above, but a strong supporting argument can be made that the eye and watchfulness of neither the Department of the Interior nor the Department of Health, Education and Welfare (should the Bureau be moved there) are strong enough to enforce the thoroughgoing prescription for improvement which the Bureau and its conduct of Indian affairs require. The form, in short, will change, but the effectiveness of application will still be less than what is needed. The effect on the Indians themselves should not be underestimated. The proposal is in line with the President's own concern for the problems of minority peoples, but, in addition, the transfer would convey to the Indians his determination to place their affairs on the highest level of governmental commitment possible and to bring to an end the problems that for so long have made them the "poorest of all poor" Americans. In proposing an independent commission or agency, the Indians were striving to extricate themselves from a submerged and unjustly competitive position in the Interior Department. A wholesale move of the Bureau to HEW would not necessarily improve their competitive position, and undoubtedly would result in generating shock waves of termination fears that would renew resistance to programs and again retard development. The transfer of the Bureau to the Executive Office of the Presidency, on the other hand, accompanied by a reorganization of the agency's structure, the resultant ending of some of the worst practices of patronage now felt particularly at the area level, and the moving of Indian affairs to other Congressional Committees and another section of the Bureau of the Budget, would inevitably provide a dramatic stimulus to Indian self-confidence and an inspiration to the invigoration of Indian initiative, motivation and energy.

The other options, though less desirable, should be mentioned:

1) The Bureau can remain in the Department of the Interior and be reorganized along the lines proposed in the next section of this study. If that occurs, the relationship of the Bureau to the rest of the Department must be changed. The Bureau is presently under the Assistant Secretary for Public Land Management, and receives short shrift both from him and from the Secretary, who are more preoccupied inevitably with questions of natural resources. Delays are

frequent, and negativism, stemming from the long delays in getting decisions from both officials, emanates back to the Bureau from the Assistant Secretary's administrative assistant, whose personal power of influence in Indian affairs is not generally recognized. At the same time, the ability of the Secretary to play a decisive role in Indian affairs is weakened when he goes through the Assistant Secretary for Public Land Management to the Commissioner of Indian Affairs. The record of the last two administrations was one of continued poor communications and "slippage" between the Secretary and the Bureau. On many occasions, the Secretary gave orders, only to discover months later that nothing had been done, or, in some cases, that the exact opposite of what he had requested had taken place. As President Truman once pointed out, this is a fact of government life, but it is a grave and often crippling flaw in the conduct of Indian affairs and will be a disadvantage in any attempt to carry out a meaningful reorganization of the Bureau of Indian Affairs within the present structure of the Department.

It is recommended, therefore, at the very least, that if the Bureau remains in the Department of the Interior, it should be placed under an Assistant Secretary for Indian and Territorial Affairs, who can give the proper attention to decision-making at the topmost level of the Department.

At the same time, delays occasioned by the Solicitor's Office of the Department must be ended. This is an administrative matter, and the Secretary himself ought to address his attention to the problem and find the methods to correct it as promptly as possible.

2) The primary responsibility for Indian affairs can be transferred to the Department of Health, Education and Welfare. If this is to be done, a re-reading of the first two sections of this study is recommended. A deliberate and careful effort will have to be made to win the Indians' understanding and agreement. The fears of termination will have to be recognized, and the Indians will have to be persuaded that their concern, not alone about termination, but that they

will be submerged and placed in a disadvantageously competitive position for services with non-Indians who greatly outnumber them, is genuinely groundless. It is questionable whether this can be guaranteed, and whether competition for programs and funding, as well as a deterioration in the recognition of the uniqueness and special position of the Indians, will not create new areas of conflicts and problems.

If the move to HEW is made, all the functions of the BIA, including education, should be transferred to a single new agency under an Assistant Secretary or, at a minimum, an Administrator, for Indian Affairs, in that Department. Practical as it may seem to the non-Indian unfamiliar with Indians, a scattering of the functions through the different branches of HEW and/or to other agencies should not occur. The shock to the tribes would be enormous, and Indian progress would come to a halt. Instead, the single new agency in HEW should be structured along the lines recommended in the next section, and its positioning in the government made thoroughly familiar to the Indians as soon as possible.

Notice should be taken of the Indians' reflection of fears of disorienting moves which they registered through the National Congress of American Indians in January, 1969, when they stated: "Indian people have *never* been successful in competing for services through other government agencies, and the services received from these agencies have been very small or practically nil. . . . Politically and socially it is almost impossible for the Indian to compete for services among other Federal agencies. . . ."

Finally, if Bureau restructuring is done effectively, it can be done as well in Interior as in HEW. Funding for the Indian agency may come easier and with more largesse in HEW than in Interior, and liaison with nearby specialized human development branches in HEW may be more effective and helpful than the long-range liaison now required between the BIA and certain branches in other agencies. But there is no necessity that requires the BIA to continue either with inadequate budgets or with inefficient liaison with other agencies simply because it is in Interior. The lack of commitment of previous administrations permitted the persistence of under-funding of Indian programs and inefficient interagency liaison, and, partly as a result of both, the legacy of Indian neglect continues to be a shameful blot in 1969.

3) The remaining option is to find the means to create an independent agency or commission, not in the Executive Office of the Presidency. This would not have the impact or commitment which Indian affairs truly require in 1969, but it would extricate the Indians from old adversaries in Congress and the Bureau of the Budget, would raise them from their present submerged position in a Department oriented toward non-Indian matters, and might place them in a better competitive position for government services available to all Americans. The proposal has never been thought out, and if it is to be pursued, full and frank discussions regarding all its ramifications should be conducted between the National Council on Indian Opportunity and the Indians who offered the proposal. . . .

V. THE BUREAU OF INDIAN AFFAIRS

The Bureau of Indian Affairs was created in the War Department in 1824 and in 1849 was transferred to the Department of the Interior. It is organized today on three levels, or echelons, that are vertically segmented by numerous Divisions grouped according to functions into Offices.

The headquarters in Washington, with about 500 of the Bureau's total 16,035 full-time employees in fiscal year '68, consists of the Office of the Commissioner (with a Deputy Commissioner, Assistants to the Commissioner, and Offices of Congressional Relations, Public Information and Inspection); three program Offices (Community Services, Economic Development and Education), each under an Assistant Commissioner; and three supporting staff Offices (Administration, Engineering and Program Coordination), each also headed by an Assistant Commissioner. The three program Offices and three supporting staff Offices each contain staff sections and a varied number of Divisions, which heavily compartmentalize the echelon and have line authority over counter-parts that similarly compartmentalize each of the other two echelons.

The intermediate level, or echelon, is that of the area offices (eleven at the time of this writing), which have broad dele-gations of authority as well as supervisory responsibility over the agencies and field installations (the third echelon) in their areas. The area offices are headed by Directors, and the echelon, as noted, is also segmented into area counterparts of the many Divisions (also known as branches) of the six pro-gram and staff Offices in Washington. Area branch officers, headed by Area Assistant Directors who are subject to their Divisions and Offices in Washington, have authority, in turn, over counterparts in the third echelon who are grouped around, but are not responsible to, the reservation, or agency, superintendent. Besides the reservations, the schools and other installations on the reservations, the third echelon in-cludes off-reservation boarding schools and independent irrigation projects administered by the Bureau.

In fiscal year '68, more than 9,000 of the Bureau's personnel and $138.2 million (55 per cent of the Bureau's $250 million budget) went into the education function. HEW's Division of Public Health employed 5,740 people for Indian health ser-vices, with a $91.3 million appropriation. Thus two-thirds of the personnel and funds expended on Indian affairs that year by the principally involved agencies went into education and health services. (The total funds appropriated for the Bureau of Indian Affairs in fiscal year '69 were $258.2 million; the amount requested in the Budget for fiscal year '70 by the Bureau is $289.1 million, which primarily reflects a $14 mil-lion increase for education and a $20 million increase for adult vocational training, certain cuts being made in other items, chiefly the construction of buildings and utilities.)

It may be argued that the decentralized structure of the Bureau, as outlined above, is necessary for good management. But, in practice, it is management for checks, balances, cau-tion, resistance and delays, and not for decisiveness and action. The "layering" and compartmentalizing, which require actions moving up and down to go sideways also, back and forth, on each layer, result inevitably in slowness, frustrations, and negativism, as well as a continuing Niagara of studies, assessments, opinions and reports. The Bureau in consequence is literally drowned in paperwork, while on the reservation level the Indians wait.

This cannot be, and is not, good management. In December, 1968, Leon Ovsiew, Professor of Educational Administration at Temple University, analyzed the administrative structure, budgeting practices and certain personnel factors of the Bureau of Indian Affairs, as they pertain to the education function, for the Senate Subcommittee on Indian Education. His study was so perceptive in pointing out the root causes of the Bureau's structural defects that, although his report referred primarily to the educational function of the Bureau, certain excerpts from it, with the alteration of a few words, should be read and re-read as being relevant to the Bureau as a whole:

The primary characteristic of a viable [Bureau organizational structure] is that leadership efforts should be both encouraged and rewarded. Though no one would be naive enough to believe that any structure alone can make leadership flourish, it is nevertheless true that structure can frustrate leadership. A good structure can do more; it can encourage good people with ideas to cast their fate with the organization for the rewards of accomplishment. In any event, if a structure actually hinders the exercise of leadership, it needs changing to a structure which encourages it. No principle of organization can be more certain.

How does the present BIA structure constrain and impede the exercise of leadership? By the quite simple process of making every idea, every experimental hypothesis, every possible adaptive change [and every programmatic or other action for decision] run the gauntlet of [area branch personnel, a generalist area director, Washington Division personnel, and an Assistant Commissioner, all of whom possess authority over the specific reservation matter in question] and whose short budgets and spending leeways make new ideas less attractive than the non-postponable functions. Forced to use an influence pattern for getting whatever consideration of their change-ideas they can, officials [wishing to move things along] must learn to lose more often than they win, and especially to lose the big ideas. It takes only a little empathy to understand the frustration this perception causes for people who know that little ideas can never hope to win the battle against the inadequacies. . . .

There is another, more subtle point about the uses of a decentralized structure. In theory, a major advantage of decentralization is that it permits a freer exercise of political democracy. Opportunities exist when administrative decisions are made close to the point of their implementation for the people affected by them to affect the decisions. . . . It would be satisfying to be able to note that such an advantage inheres in the BIA administrative structure. But the route upward through the echelons seems to be no less difficult than downward for personnel, at least on the things that matter most. The BIA's philosophy of organization derogates the [grassroots Indians, specialists and coordinating administrator in favor of echelons of administrators and absentee specialists higher up].

The BIA structure is designed more than most for stability. It is doubtful that very much could be done with or to the people in the organization, given the present structure, to encourage innovative practice. . . . One thing does seem certain: the present structure not only serves to reward unaggressive behavior and docility but punishes, usually by transfer, those who persist in behaving like leaders. The reward system of BIA discourages leadership, on purpose. *It is, therefore, not possible to conceive of change and improvement within the present structure.* (Italics added.)

These findings, to repeat, were addressed primarily to the organization of the Bureau's educational system, but they apply with equal vividness to the Bureau's entire structure. On the reservation level, where Indians are trying to participate constructively to help frame, design and execute programs to meet their problems, they are hamstrung and frustrated daily by an endless round of delays and negativism occasioned by the internal workings of the higher echelons of the Bureau. The effect is that the Indians cannot participate in making decisions for themselves, for in meaningful things, the decisions cannot be made at their level. Government protestations in support of the principle of self-determination notwithstanding, the important decisions must be, and are, made — under the present arrangement — in the echelons above the Indians.

Such a system, as noted, defeats the personnel within the system. There are undoubtedly weak, poor, and inefficient men within the Bureau. Some enter the system, especially at the area level, by patronage: some should never have been employed by the Bureau; some are poor because of inadequate training and orientation after they were employed; and some were good originally but, after many frustrations and defeats, gave up. The Office of Inspection in the Commissioner's Office, which is charged with the obligation to "identify and correct any operational weakness which might reflect upon the efficiency or integrity of the Bureau," gives little evidence of ability or determination to carry out its mission. One of the scores of "weaknesses," with which it appears unable to cope, is the continued presence within the Bureau of key personnel who long since should have been removed from it. The Commissioners themselves should bear a large portion of the blame for not having found the means by which to remove inadequate personnel. Indian children are being emotionally disabled for life by the ignorance of unfit people in the Bureau's educational system. Many members of Indian communities are driven to desperation, some even to suicide, as a result of ineptitude, indifference or lethargy on the part of a poor superintendent or area official. Yet the record of the 1960's contains documentation of Commissioner Nash turning down Indian appeals to relieve them of intolerable agency personnel by telling them that he would not remove a man while he was under fire, and of Commissioner Bennett answering tribal compaints of frustration and negativism with the retort that he was not interested in discussing "criticism of the BIA." The self-evident fact that the Commissioner and the Office of Inspection have not acted determinedly in this matter is an added reason for transferring the Bureau to the Executive Office of the Presidency, where some of the unspoken forces that presently account for the Commissioner's inhibitions, including the pressure of patronage demands and the rigid dicta of Civil Service—neither of which should be viewed as anything but evil when the lives and health of American citizens, and especially children, are at stake—can be better dealt with.

At the same time, it should be recognized that the Bureau contains many more persons with exceptional ability and talent and a high degree of dedication. When the Indians criticize them, they are, in truth, criticizing a structure that binds and frustrates its personnel. That such persons remain in the Bureau and continue to do their best is a testament to the intensity of their commitment. "Many, many inspired people in the service have lived in hope, and died in despair, trying their level best to help the Indian people take their rightful place in America," W. W. Keeler told Secretary Udall in 1961, when his Task Force was about to begin its work.

Neither that Task Force, nor any of those that followed it, made the proposal which this study now believes is mandatory, namely that:

Wherever the present Bureau of Indian Affairs is positioned within the government, its structure must be thoroughly reorganized.

The form of that reorganization must satisfy two principal goals: a) it must end the Bureau's present defects that have been noted above; and b) it must achieve the transfer of a maximum of technical services, facilities and decision-making capabilities to the reservation level, face to face with the Indians.

At the present time, a decision for a meaningful proposal that originates after a meeting between the Indians and a branch officer on the reservation faces a long, torturous route: from the branch officer to the agency superintendent to the area branch officer to the area assistant director to the area director to the Division in Washington to the Assistant Commissioner to the Commissioner, and perhaps higher still. Eventually, it starts down again, following the same zigzag route. Even this is a simplified version, for it may be side-tracked at any step along the way into the offices of other branches and to solicitors.

The recommendations made to the Commissioner of Indian Affairs during the self-examination of the Bureau in 1965–66 and those that were made in January, 1969, by the National Congress of American Indians reflected an experienced, reservation-based awareness of why things happened as they did. The malpractices that they were intended to correct were many, but one example will suffice. In the budget process, each agency, in theory, prepares its own budget, which is then evaluated by the area office and consolidated into an area budget, then submitted to the Washington office for similar evaluation and consolidation. In practice, guidelines based upon previous budgets are determined in Washington, and allocations are actually dictated and controlled by the Divisions as entities rather than by the agencies at the operational level. For example, if a superintendent decides that the budget of one branch on his reservation should be cut and another increased in order to serve a tribe more effectively, the offended branch sends word up through the line to its Division chief in Washington, who then informs the superintendent that if his branch does not need the money in his agency, it will be transferred within the same branch to another agency. Under this system, considerable time and energy that should be spent on service at the operational level are expended in conflicts between the Division hierarchies on the one hand, and the superintendents and area directors on the other. At the same time, the system often results in the presence on reservations of branch specialists who are not needed and, conversely, of not enough personnel or funding for branches that are badly needed. No wonder the National Congress of American Indians asked for the granting of veto power to tribal governing bodies during the local agency budget submittal process and "the reorganization of agencies to change the present structure, which calls for an agency branch to complement every Washington branch chief, whether or not it is needed on a particular reservation, and to include an effective combination of facilities and services for that reservation"!

> *It is recommended, therefore, that the reorganization of the structure of the Bureau . . . include:*
> —*the elimination of the Offices of the Assistant Commissioners for Community Services and Economic Development, together with all the staffs and Divisions of those Offices;*
> —*the readjustment of the present Offices of the Assistant Commissioners for Administration, Engineering and Program Coordination as guidance, coordinating, budgeting, administration and management arms of the Bureau, reporting to the Commissioner;*
> —*a separate structure for the Assistant Commissioner for Education, who would report to the Commissioner, but would retain his present staffs and Divisions, and would have direct line authority to all elements of the educational system, as well as coordinators with area and agency programs, tribes, and state and local school systems;*
> —*the addition of regional coordinating desk officers, reporting to the Commissioner, but without line authority;*
> —*the addition of an Office of Urban Indian Affairs, concerned with the problems of urban Indians and reporting to the Commissioner;*
> —*the retention of area offices headed by Assistant Commissioners, but the elimination of all branches at the area level and the reorientation of the area office's function to that of providing guidance, advice and assistance to reservations; and*
> —*the focusing of primary operational attention on the reservations by placing all specialists, save those in education, on the reservation and giving the superintendent authority over them and their budgeting, and a direct line via the area Assistant Commissioner to the Office of the Commissioner.*

This system would eliminate all but one of the conflicting branch hierarchies and give the agency superintendent the line authority, responsibility and flexibility essential for effective operations at the service level. Changing the title of Area Director to Assistant Commissioner for a given area would enhance the line of authority from the Commissioner to the operational level and would discourage the additional interposition at the Washington office of line officers between the Commissioner and the field. (The miscellaneous agencies now reporting direct to Washington should be assigned to an Assistant Commissioner for the East and Southeast, and the Mississippi Choctaw Agency should probably be transferred to this jurisdiction.)

Regional desk officers in the Commissioner's office would have no line authority. Their function would be to keep abreast of programs and developments in the field, area by area, thus serving the Commissioner as a constantly available source of coordinated information on relative progress among the areas, as well as providing background for evaluating new developments.

The retention of an Assistant Commissioner for Education and the transfer of the school system and other education services, as well as the Institute of American Indian Arts, which now reports to the Commissioner's Office, to his separate line of authority must have high priority attention. It will provide for the first time the structure needed to reform the Indian educational system and allow the unified planning of policies and the execution of professionally planned programs. It will permit the establishment of uniform educational standards and a unified administration of them. At the same time, it will relieve the superintendents and area directors of extremely burdensome administrative problems relating to the Bureau schools, educational services and public school relations, for which they have no professional training, and will permit them to concentrate on tribal development programs. Potential hazards that might stem from this separation can be met by giving the Assistant Commissioner coordinators with area and agency programs, and the Area Assistant Commissioners and agency superintendents education liaison officers, as indicated.

The assignment at the area level of technicians and survey teams, as also indicated, would help to solve the problem of permanent staffs of technicians who languish at agencies where their services are only seasonally or temporarily needed (i.e., foresters). Buildings and their maintenance could be taken over by the tribes under contract (this is already being done in at least one area). Needed new buildings could be supplied by the tribes, working through the General Services Administration, using money borrowed on the basis of long-term rental contracts. Consideration should be given as to whether the agencies should retain the authority for making such arrangements for school buildings, as well as other Bureau plants. . . .

On the reservations, the reorganization will bring about a new set of relations. The Indians will truly be encouraged to work up programs for themselves with the cooperation of the superintendent and the aid of specialists. They will be in a new position, one in which they will be able to play a decisive role in the framing of the agency budget, based entirely on reservation needs, and to submit the budget for review and coordination in Washington, as they have wished. The layering and compartmentalizing that now deadens initiative and energies on the reservations will have disappeared, and the Indians, in fact, will have been unfettered.

In addition to Bureau reorganization, the following recommendations are also made:

— *The National Council on Indian Opportunity, which has already proved its value, should be continued, with its present functions adequately funded;*

— *Training programs, and adequate orientation seminars in Indian (and tribal) history and cultures, should be set up and carried out systematically for Bureau personnel who work at every level of the Bureau;*

— *Superintendents, area heads, and the new Office concerned with urban Indian affairs should be directed to seek from the tribes and Indian communities the most effective methods by which information about government programs can be communicated to the individual Indians. A crippling* problem on many reservations, as well as off reservations, is that many Indians do not know what programs are available to them (for education, welfare, economic development, etc.) and do not know how to go about getting help that they need and that actually could be given to them. It should be a prime function of the Information Office of the Bureau to get such information to the entire Indian population and, with the help of the Indians themselves and the field officers of the BIA, arrive at the most effective ways to circulate that information with maximum "reader impact." For instance, the radio and television media might be used more effectively than they are now.

—*Contracts with tribes must be accompanied by improved payment procedures, a continuity of planning and programming, the ending of unnecessary supervision and requirements, the provision of necessary working capital and equipment, and an agreement that tribes should receive a fair return, not be required to pay sub-standard wages, and be offered projects that will require them to develop their own staffs of skilled personnel.* In this regard, it should be noted that some tribes badly need the means by which they can hire permanent employees (i.e., a tribal business manager or executive secretary) to provide a continuity of development and to service programs. This lack of continuity in some tribal governments has been another obstacle to the growth of initiative and to economic development. It would be a breakthrough if budgeting could provide for the tribal hiring of the Indians' own needed technical or professional employees. Priority might be given for one such employee apiece to be provided to those small and impoverished tribal groups that have been so completely stymied by this lack.

—*Attention should be given, and steps taken, to end the Bureau's deficiencies in the field of research and development; in the lack of meaningful and adequate data on Indians and Indian affairs; in the use of consultants and non-govern-*

ment experts; and in the modernization of its administrative, fiscal, record-keeping, and other management practices.

—Indian Affairs should be headed by an Indian, but he should possess all the qualities of dedication, determination, knowledge and vigor that the leadership of the federal conduct of Indian affairs now requires. Indians should also be placed in as many policy- and decision-making positions within the Bureau as possible. Moreover, if the Bureau is kept within the Department of the Interior, the Secretary should have an Indian staff assistant primarily responsible for liaison with the new Assistant Secretary for Indian and Territorial Affairs, the BIA, and Indian affairs generally.

VI. PROGRAMMATIC RECOMMENDATIONS

It is certain that the worst problems afflicting American Indians will never be ended without programs that are adequately funded. It is accepted that the Indians do not have the funds themselves and that they do not have access to the sources of credit that are usually available to other Americans. But the actual funding of programs for Indians by the government has never approached the level required by the massive dimensions of the problems.

A few of the facts obscured by the promulgation of intentions in President Johnson's Message on Indian Affairs on March 6, 1968, underscore the point. The Message conveyed proposals for many new or expanded programs which, somehow, were to be financed by only a ten per cent increase in federal expenditures for Indians above the appropriations of the previous year. One of the proposals was for a ten per cent increase in funds for health programs, including a number of items that would make available to the Indians greater numbers of trained personnel to help cope with the many serious health problems on the reservations. Before the year was over, the exact opposite had come to pass, and the Public Health Service was pointing out that, under Section 201 of the Revenue and Expenditure Control Act of 1968, Public Law 90–364, the Division of Indian Health was facing a reduction of almost 1,000 employees, or one-sixth of its total staff, principally among nursing personnel and other patient care supportive staff in the field. A reduction in staff is now occurring on reservations and in Indian hospitals, not only nullifying the promise held out in President Johnson's Message, but bringing a new crisis to the Indians. (Corrective legislation, it hardly needs pointing out, is required at the earliest possible moment.)

Again, the inadequacy of funding a program to deal effectively with another pressing problem is evidenced in the field of Indian housing. The Presidential Task Force had reported to the White House that at least three-quarters of all Indian houses on reservations were below minimum standards of decency and that over a 10-year period roughly 100,000 units, "of which approximately 80,000 are new, would have to be provided for the housing needs of the Indian population." The President's response to the Task Force's assertion that this would require a 10-year program costing approximately $1 billion was to propose an increase of only 1,000 new Indian homes (for a total of 2,500) to be built under HUD programs in fiscal year '69.

The American taxpayer may wonder with increasing impatience why Indian problems are not solved, and why expenditures for those problems continue to mount each year. One demonstrable answer is that the expenditures have never been high enough to do much more than keep the problems going. In the years after the Indians' pacification, the appropriations barely met the minimum subsistence needs of the Indians. In more recent years, with an increasing Indian population and a growing complexity of reservation problems, the appropriations have risen, but consistently have stayed well below a level needed to carry out intentions. It may be impossible, because of higher priority needs elsewhere in the federal budget and the consequent requirement for economy in the Indian budget, to attempt to solve the Indians' problems once and for all with the same kind of massive appropriations that have characterized the most ambitious aid programs for some of the underdeveloped peoples overseas. But it should be emphasized that the Indians are Americans, and that until a similar approach is adopted for them, Indian programs will continue to limp along, and Indian development will proceed at an unsatisfactory pace. In addition, because of the rapid increase in the Indians' population, there is every prospect that their economic, educational and health levels will drop steadily behind those of the rest of the population, and that each Administration will leave the Indians worse off, in relation to the rest of the American people, than it found them.

Adequate funding, therefore, should be a major concern of every Indian program. . . .

The planning and application of all economic development programs, long- and short-range, should reflect the Indians' own needs, desires and cultural traits. By bringing the Indians into the planning and decision-making process, programs need not fail, as they have in the past. . . .

With minor exceptions, the Indians desire the federal government to continue to provide its trust protection for their lands, and the government must continue to give that protection. But it should be possible, by amending the Indian Reorganization Act and other pertinent statutes, to reduce the number of ancillary obligations and responsibilities of the trustee. In their drive for self-determination and self-government, tribes will press increasingly for the right to program their judgment funds, have authority over their budgets, and assume full responsibility for the management of their income, the making of contracts with attorneys, and the framing of tribal codes, resolutions, and constitutional actions. Without abandoning the trusteeship protection of lands, the government should be in a position to be able to transfer those other responsibilities, piecemeal or in full, to tribes deemed ready to assume them. For some tribes, that day may already have arrived, and the continued denial to them of rights they are able to exercise for themselves may be viewed as the most stultifying of all the obstacles that inhibit them on their road to development.

"OUR BROTHER'S KEEPER"

The Citizens' Advocate Center
October, 1969

The Josephy report to President Nixon focused attention on certain technical aspects of federal-Indian relations that had been impeding the attainment of self-determination. These included the primary responsibility of the Bureau of Indian Affairs to congressional committees and the Bureau of the Budget, both of which were hostile toward Indian self-determination; the conflict of interest within the Department of the Interior when Indian rights and needs clashed with other interests represented or protected by Interior; and the structural defects within the Bureau of Indian Affairs, which effectively precluded tribal self-determination.

In the Congress, members of the Interior committees predictably opposed that section of the report that examined the transfer of Indian affairs to another place in the government, for they did not wish to lose control of the Indians. Among the Indians themselves, the reactions to the report were mixed. Some of them, particularly urban Indians and young activists who saw the Bureau of Indian Affairs as a tyrannical—or, at best, patronizing—bureaucracy and as the principal tormentor of the Indians, quickened their demand for the total abolition of the BIA and the transfer of all its powers to the Indians. Within the BIA, Indians, who filled many thousands of the lower-paid menial and non-policy-making positions in the bureau, responded in alarm. Few of them saw the report, but rumor told them that it advocated the abolition of the BIA, and their non-Indian superiors in the agency, even more concerned over the threat to their own status quo, encouraged their fear for their jobs.

On the reservations tribal reactions varied. Many Indian leaders proposed more study and consideration. The tribal representatives serving on the Executive Committee of the National Congress of American Indians voted in favor of discouraging proposals to abolish the Bureau of Indian Affairs or disperse its services among other government agencies, but they called for legislation to make the bureau an independent commission or agency.

In October, 1969, the annual convention of the National Congress of American Indians, held in Albuquerque, New Mexico, voted firmly against any shift of the Bureau of Indian Affairs out of the Department of the Interior, giving its reasons as follows:

1) Any failures of the bureau in the past were due in the main to interferences in operation by higher authorities within the Department of the Interior and by congressional statements of policy, with inadequate appropriations to assure sustained progress.

2) The detachment of the bureau from the Department of the Interior could lead to restatement of policy and principles, such as attended the transfer of Indian health to Health, Education and Welfare, but on a wider and more devastating scale in reference to treaty and other fundamental rights.

3) Indians tribally and individually are making progress and we feel assured that this progress could be further stimulated and accelerated by the proper reorientation of executive authority in a reorganization of the Department of the Interior in respect to Indian Affairs.

An explanation of the various pressures and fears that lay behind this stand by the tribal delegates to the National Congress of American Indians was provided that same month with the publication of a book titled *Our Brother's Keeper: The Indian in White America.* The volume was the result of a study initiated by Edgar S. Cahn, a Washington, D.C., lawyer who was interested in the lack of accountability of government bodies, particularly those administering programs for the poor and powerless, to the beneficiaries of the programs. With funds raised by his organization, the Citizens' Advocate Center, Cahn's research and writing staff, composed of Indians and non-Indians, produced a report that on publication created a stir both within and outside the government and intensified the impact on the administration of much that had been stated in the February report to the President.

The volume's detailed examination of the injustices to which Indians were still being subjected by the white man and his government raised the blood pressure of readers; its conclusions, confirming situations highlighted in the earlier report to President Nixon, made clear again the lack of responsibility of the BIA, the Department of the Interior, the Bureau of the Budget, the Congress, or any agency of government to the Indians.

One of the chapters, "The Bureau of Indian Affairs: The Lesser of Two Evils," illuminated tribal feelings about the bureau. It showed, in portions like those that follow, the reasons why many tribes — despite their own continued attacks on the BIA — feared the white men's attacks on, or tampering with, the agency, and why they opposed suggestions for moving it out of the Interior Department.

The Indian tolerates his present impotent and unjust status in his relations with the Federal Government because he sees the Bureau of Indian Affairs as the lesser of two evils. The BIA is all he has, and every promise to replace it with something better has been broken.

Those new to Indian problems and enraged by the conduct of the BIA, and even those long acquainted with the Bureau's impenetrable bureaucracy, often reach an obvious conclusion: why not just do away with the Bureau and, in the words of a U.S. Senator, "free" the Indians?

The easy answer is the wrong answer, and the Indian knows it better than anyone else. Those who would abolish the Bureau to "help" the Indian will find as their most vehement opponent the Indian himself. He knows that he must, even at the cost of his liberty, preserve the Bureau—because the Bureau and only the Bureau stands between the Indian and extinction as a racial and cultural entity. Only the Bureau stands between the Indian and total, unilateral renunciation of all federal treaty obligations. The Bureau has been and the Bureau remains the special protector of the Indian and his champion, at times, against predatory interests. The Bureau and the solemn promises of the Federal Government are symbolically synonomous in the mind of the Indian. To destroy one is to destroy both.

The Bureau has done a terrible job; it has compromised the Indian time and again; it has permitted, tolerated, even assisted in the erosion of Indian rights and the whittling away of the Indian land base. Still, to the Indian, it is *his*. In the light of wisdom gained from long years of bitter experience, the Indian knows that a threat to the Bureau, an attack on the Bureau or any change in its structure is to be resisted as a threat to his own survival. . . .

. . . those who try to make changes in the Bureau will find themselves met with substantial opposition from Indians. . . . Indians can and often do criticize the Bureau, but they do not necessarily regard the non-Indian critic as an ally. They know that criticism can play directly into the hands of their worst enemies — those who wish to end the special relationship which exists between the Indian and the Federal Government.

Even the truth is to be resisted, if it is a truth which can endanger their protector, the Bureau. The Bureau plays upon this fear to stimulate Indians, and particularly tribal leaders, to attack and deny any report which seeks to tell the truth — although the same Indians privately will admit the truth of the charges, and even cite examples.

The Indian not only tolerates the injustice of the system; he helps insulate it from scrutiny and criticism, because history has convinced him that an attack on the Bureau will lead to the destruction of his special status as an Indian, and to the death of his people.

"WE SPEAK AS INDIANS"

American Indian Task Force
Washington, D.C., November, 1969

Our Brother's Keeper was essentially a revelation of conditions and it contained no recommendations. Prior to its publication, Edgar Cahn won endorsement for the study's findings from a group of Indian leaders of various ages, interests, and tribal affiliations, and as an Indian Editorial Board they served as sponsors for the book when it was issued.

The next step, in the view of the Citizens' Advocate Center, was for Indians to decide for themselves what, if anything, they wished to do with the report. With the center's assistance, the Indian Editorial Board was turned into a so-called American Indian Task Force and enlarged to forty-two members. The roster of the task force, comprising many of the best-known Indian leaders in the country, included the following persons:

Earl Old Person, Chairman, Blackfeet Tribe; President, National Congress of American Indians

Jess Six Killer, Cherokee; Executive Director, American Indians United

George Groundhog, Cherokee; Director, Original Cherokee Community Organization

Viola Hatch, Cheyenne-Arapaho; field worker, Oklahomans for Indian Opportunity

Dennis J. Banks, Chippewa; Director, American Indian Movement

Clyde Bellecourt, Chippewa; President, American Indian Movement

Ted Holappa, Chippewa; Executive Director, American Indian Cultural Center, Los Angeles

Simon Howard, Chippewa

Roger Jourdain, Chairman, Red Lake Chippewa; Regional Vice President, NCAI

Lucy Covington, Colville tribal councilwoman

H. Miles Brandon, Eskimo; member, Alaska Federation of Natives

Margaret Nick, Eskimo

D'Arcy McNickle, Flathead

Thomas Banyacya, Hopi

Douglas L. Sakiestewa, Hopi-Navajo

James Wahpepah, Chairman, Kickapoo Tribal Council; President, Oklahomans for Indian Opportunity

John Belindo, Kiowa-Navajo; Executive Director, NCAI

Mary Cornelius, Chairman, Little Shell Tribe of Turtle Mountain Chippewa

Monroe M. Weso, Menominee

Wendell Chino, Chairman, Mescalero Apache Tribal Council; former President, NCAI

Bernard Second, Mescalero Apache

Peterson Zah, Navajo

Peter MacDonald, Navajo; Executive Director, Office of Navajo Economic Opportunity

Dr. Taylor McKenzie, Navajo

Janet McCloud, Tulalip

Ernie Stevens, Oneida; Executive Director, Intertribal Council of California

Charles H. Lohah, Osage

Cipriano Manuel, Papago

Archie J. LaCoote, Passamaquoddy

Al Elgin, Pomo; Executive Director, Intertribal Friendship House, Oakland, California

William Pensoneau, Ponca; President, National Indian Youth Council

Martha Grass, Ponca

Seferino Tenerio, Pueblo

James Vidovich, Chairman, Pyramid Lake Paiutes

Kesley Edmo, Shoshone

E. Ray Briggs, Sioux

Johnson Holy Rock, Sioux

Cato Valandra, former chairman, Rosebud Sioux

Paul Bernal, Taos Pueblo

Rose Crow Flies High, Three Affiliated Tribes

Francis McKinley, Ute; member, Far West Laboratory for Educational Research

Angelo LaMere, Winnebago; member of Great Lakes Intertribal Council

In November, 1969, members of the Indian Task Force met in Washington, pondered principally the book's major theme regarding the lack of governmental accountability to the Indians, and developed a new approach toward Indian self-determination. On November 12 the Indians met in the White House with Vice President Spiro Agnew and various presidential assistants and presented a statement that incorporated their new idea. Two days later, at the Capitol, they read to members of Congress and the Washington press another statement expanding on Indian grievances and calling for a new day for the tribes. Excerpts from both statements, making clear what these diverse Indian leaders had agreed upon, follow.

THE TASK FORCE'S STATEMENT PRESENTED TO VICE
PRESIDENT SPIRO AGNEW AND WHITE HOUSE STAFF
NOVEMBER 10, 1969

We speak as Indians who care about what has happened to our people. We speak out because every individual must, and there must be some who are willing to start a process. We do not view ourselves as "chosen leaders" or an "Indian elite," though we come from various backgrounds and diverse tribes. But we do claim to be a cross-section of concerned non-establishment Indians.

We came together initially to assist in providing information for the book *Our Brother's Keeper* and to state whether, within our own personal knowledge, it spoke the truth.

The national concern aroused by *Our Brother's Keeper* cannot be allowed to dissipate. One of the main points made by this book is that, unlike most Americans, the Indians have little or no forum for redress of grievances and wrongs committed against them. The Task Force believes that there must be a direct channel of communication so that Indian voices are not lost in the Bureau of Indian Affairs, the Department of Interior, the Bureau of the Budget, Congressional Committees, or other parts of the bureaucratic and political maze in which Indians are now trapped. We are, therefore, proposing a process which could provide a way in which Indians could speak directly to the government of the United States, both to seek a redress of grievances and to initiate and shape Indian policy. . . .

The Task Force proposes that a process of dialogue be initiated in all areas which shall coincide with the eleven area offices of the Bureau of Indian Affairs.

Each of these eleven areas is partially represented by individual members of the Task Force but it would be the responsibility of the entire Task Force, working with others, to expand in each area to insure that it included a broad spectrum of representation from numerous tribes, tribal chairmen, local organizations, individual spokesmen involved in issues, and representatives of urban Indians from cities within each area. Thus, the Task Force will establish separate and broadly representative Boards of Inquiry which would conduct hearings, receive grievances, and generate recommendations in the manner set forth below.

1. That a working meeting of the Task Force, with the National Council on Indian Opportunity, be convened to determine the best way to present the idea of conferences and hearings.

2. That further area conferences be held to explain the need to begin the hearing process with each area's representatives to the Task Force and NCIO to discuss ways to expand the concept and lay groundwork for the hearings.

3. That there be hearings in each of the eleven areas—these hearings are to take testimony in open meetings from groups, tribes, and individuals about the needs and situations of the various people and to call for specific recommendations from the people. We urge federal agencies to attend the hearings as observers.

A. After the hearings, there will be continued input into the process through complaint and evaluation process by having a local center or person to take complaints in each local community. A "circuit rider" is to be hired by the local Board of Inquiry who will take the complaints and make recommendations about solutions.

B. Red ribbon "grand juries," composed entirely of Indians, should be convened in order to investigate and report upon deprivations of rights, charges of inaction or unresponsiveness by officials, lack of effectiveness of educational, health and other services—and . . . where the facts appear to warrant it, the red ribbon "grand jury" shall not only come forward with findings of fact, but should also, by prior arrangement with the U.S. Attorney, present an "indictment" which the U.S. Attorney, or (in the event of conflict of interest) a lawyer provided by the government shall be called upon to investigate such charges and represent Indians in such a manner as to protect their rights and make government programs genuinely responsive to the desires and needs of Indians.

4. The Boards of Inquiry in the eleven areas are to meet again to evaluate the first round of hearings, include the continuing complaints, consider the circuit rider's findings, and take recommendation from another round of testimony to deal particularly with proposals and recommendations.

5. From each of the hearings and Boards of Inquiry, there is to be a National Board of Inquiry, composed of three members from each of the eleven areas to meet and make national recommendations. These members are to be chosen by an elective process by Indians. Finally, the entire process will result in the creation of a permanent ongoing local watchdog on bureaucratic programs.

We make this proposal because as Indians, we choose to go beyond talking about process and dialogue and consultation and to try to think through what would be a process that would be honest and would give Indians a genuine opportunity to be heard, to seek a redress of grievances and to take the initiative in shaping government policy.

We propose that the Task Force, supplemented by additional Indians from additional tribes and organizations, form a core of a group which would contract to implement this proposal. We believe that the time has come, not only for Indians to be consulted, but for them to design and implement a process of consultation whereby they can speak out their own grievances as they know them, articulate their problems, shape proposals, draft recommendations, circulate proposed legislative or administrative action for widespread discussion among Indian peoples. We believe that such functions should be performed by Indians — that there is no question here as to whether qualified Indians exist when this proposal has come from Indians — and we believe there is a clear statutory duty to contract this function to Indians under 36 Stat. L. 861. We submit that this is not only desirable — but that it would be a major symbolic break with the past practice where no Indians have been the ones paid to become Indian experts, while Indians served as volunteer educators for non-

Indians.

We do not come here to blame this administration for the failures of the past—it is our hope that by implementing a listening process, that another group like this, in some future time, will not be needed because this administration failed to hear the Indian peoples.

PRESS STATEMENT TO CONGRESS MADE BY AMERICAN
INDIAN TASK FORCE
NOVEMBER 12, 1969

I. We, the first Americans, come to the Congress of the United States that you give us the chance to try to solve what you call the Indian problem. You have had two hundred years and you have not succeeded by your standards. It is clear that you have not succeeded in ours.

On Monday, we asked the Vice President of the United States to set into motion a process which would insure that our people could secure redress of grievances and could shape the government programs that affect and control their lives. . . .

We have asked the Vice President of the United States for Indian boards of inquiries which would hold hearings throughout the areas where Indians live, for area conferences, for red ribbon grand juries, for circuit riders to take complaints and for a National Board of Inquiry to meet and make national recommendations based upon the complaints and recommendations received on the grass roots level.

And we ask you to help us see that the process we proposed to the Vice President somehow becomes a reality. We hope that he will be willing to do it on his own. But we ask you, as the representatives of the people of the United States, to serve as our representatives too—to help us see that assurances do not become empty promises. And, if necessary, to enact legislation which will create such a process where Indians can really shape government policy and control their own lives and destinies if that is not done by the Executive Branch.

II. We come to you with a sense of impending betrayal at

150

a moment when we wish to seek redress of grievances to ask you to broaden our access to the courts to protect the rights guaranteed us by your treaties and statutes. And we find, with a sense of horror, and impending doom, that instead, the Congress of the United States is on the verge of passing an Amendment to the Economic Opportunity Act which would effectively diminish the slight access to the courts we have gained in recent years through the advent of the OEO Legal Service Program. And it is an even greater irony that we find this to be the case when a governor's veto in at least one state has already killed a legal service program for Indians. What right do the governors have to interfere with what goes on on the reservation? What right do state governors have to interfere with the solemn promises made to us by the federal government in statutes and treaties which can only be enforced by resort to the courts? What right do you, or any generation of Americans, have to rip up the solemn promises of the past—promises made to us both by the Constitution and by the President of a nation which still holds and enjoys the land received in exchange for those treaties? There are none among you who would suggest that rights—and above all the right to petition one's government—can have any meaning at all without lawyers and without access to the forum where the people traditionally petition their government.

III. We come to you today to ask that you set your own house in order. We say that until the congressional committees which control nearly all Indian legislation cease to be hostile to the interests of the Indian, then we have been deprived of one of the three branches of what we have been repeatedly told is our government as well as yours.

The present committees have pushed for termination, and have fostered on Congress seemingly neutral and technical legislation, under the guise of Indian expertise, which has taken away our land, our water rights, our mineral resources and handed them over to the white man.

You have been duped—as we have been duped. These committees have created a monstrous bureaucracy insensitive to Indians which trembles and cringes before them. The Indian suffers—and the nation pays the bill. Nothing will change so long as this unholy alliance exists between the BIA and these Congressional Committees.

On Monday we asked the Vice President to seek a new arrangement within the Executive Branch of Government—one which will by-pass those channels which are hostile and insensitive to our interests. We asked him to set in motion a process by which our voices could be heard on our needs within the Executive Branch of Government.

Today, we come to seek a new arrangement with the Congress. We have come to seek a change in the committees that deal in Indian affairs. We ask that the committees of Congress not be dominated by interests which are hostile to our own survival. We ask that these committees act as a watchdog on federal programs which are passed especially for our benefit but which do not in fact benefit us because of the way the BIA runs them. And, we ask that these committees insure that we get our fair share of general legislation. We do not get our fair share of these programs now. And we do not have any means to seek redress when the very programs that are passed to help us in fact are used as means to enslave and oppress us.

We come here today to remind you that you are not just the representatives of local districts or of states. You are members of the Congress of the United States. You have national obligations. We know you are highly conscious of your national obligations when you deliberate on such problems as the war in Viet Nam. We know that you have even taken those obligations seriously enough to go to Viet Nam in order to personally inform yourself on how the Executive carries out the commitments of the United States.

We ask that you do no less at home—for the United States has made older and more sacred national commitments to the people who have occupied these shores for twenty-five thousand years. The United States has made national commitments in the form of treaties, legislation and the Constitution, itself, to our peoples. We ask you to come to our homes—in the cities and on the reservations. We ask that you seek with equal vigilance to determine whether national commitments have been kept to us. Guided tours by bureaucrats will only serve to hamper you in your search for truth.

You, the Congress of the United States, are being asked to come to see how we really live and to try to understand the values, the culture and the way of life we are fighting to preserve—an American way of life. A way of life which we believe is built upon respect for differences, a tolerance of diversity.

We cannot come to Washington. We are not rich. And we cannot afford the high price of democracy.

In essence, we ask the restoration of what you claimed at the founding of your nation—the inalienable right to pursue happiness. We cannot fail worse than the experts and the bureaucrats. We do not lack for knowledge—and we are not ashamed to hire experts and technicians. But our people do not lack for leaders, for sensitivity, for talent and ability. We ask for the right to pursue our dream—and we ask for you to respect that dream. That is the American way. We claim our birthright.

STATEMENT OF THE UNITED SOUTHEASTERN TRIBES—1969

In February, 1969, the study written for the White House had recommended transferring Indian affairs to the Executive Office of the Presidency for the higher priority, mandate, and increased visibility that such a move would bring to the Indians and their needs and desires. Although it gave serious consideration to the proposal, the Nixon Administration decided early against it, preferring to leave the Bureau of Indian Affairs, for the time being at least, in the Department of the Interior, where most tribes also wished it to remain.

By the fall of 1969, however, the real center of governmental direction of Indian affairs was—temporarily, at least—making a subtle shift to the White House. On the one hand, presidential assistants under the President's aide, Leonard Garment, were overseeing the preparation of the administration's Indian policy, which, with implementing programs, would not be ready for public announcement, as it turned out, until July, 1970. On the other hand, the Vice President was giving active leadership and considerable personal attention to the National Council on Indian Opportunity, which was centered in his office. That body, created by a Presidential Executive Order on March 6, 1968, was headed by the Vice President and consisted of seven Cabinet members and six Indian members appointed by the President for two-year terms. Its purposes were to help coordinate all federal programs affecting Indians, to involve Indians in the highest levels of the federal policy and program formulative process, and to act as trouble-shooter in the whole spectrum of Indian affairs.

Increasingly, Indians found themselves going to the White House to take their ideas and problems to Leonard Garment's assistants or to the staff of the National Council on Indian Opportunity, or to both of them. This development, together with certain other forces also at work, had the effect of almost immobilizing the field operations of the Bureau of Indian Affairs. For one thing, the knowledge that a new Indian policy was being worked out by administration men at the White House led to a stalling attitude about Indian affairs at the Department of the Interior, which was felt, in turn, by the Bureau of Indian Affairs. As if that were not enough, the interest in Indian affairs by top officials of the Interior Department had every reason to wither, since the Public Land Law Review Commission, certain influential members of Congress, and administration planners themselves were seriously examining the possible conversion of the Department of the Interior into a Department of Natural Resources. If that came about, as the Public Land Law Review Commission actually did recommend in 1970, there was a possibility that Indian affairs, or a major part of them, would be transferred somewhere else and would no longer be the responsibility of the department.

In view of all the straws blowing in the wind, the Secretary of the Interior, recognizing the need to wait until the administration's plans were more firmly settled, paid little attention to Indian matters, and Bureau of Indian Affairs personnel in the field found themselves receiving scant attention, direction, or support. The administration's new Commissioner of Indian Affairs, Louis Bruce, an Indian of Mohawk-Sioux ancestry and a successful businessman who had lived in New York City, busied himself getting to know the Indians' problems and making plans for changes in the bureau's structure and procedures that would transform it from a management to a service organization. As a first step toward "Indianizing" the bureau, he appointed all-Indian task forces to prepare programs for making the bureau more responsive to the needs of the Indians, for carrying out bureau policies and programs more effectively, and for developing Indian administrators and managers for the bureau. One result, in October, 1970, was the "realignment" of top executive positions in the bureau and the naming of fifteen Indians to key executive posts. But by and large, as the planning work in Washington proceeded, few of the tribes felt any change in their relations with the bureau, and through the first year and a half of the Nixon administration self-determination as an accepted principle and fact still seemed far from realization.

Meanwhile, changes on another front began to alarm the tribes. In line with economy and executive agency reorganization plans, the administration and Congress proposed moves that threatened the continuation of certain federal programs that had been started by the Johnson administration and had been benefiting the Indians as well as elements of the non-Indian population. Some of the programs—economic, educational, legal, social, and technical in nature—were to be curtailed, while others would be handed over to the states.

To the Indians, the proposed changes meant more than the curtailment or hobbling of programs that had been aiding their material progress. A number of the programs had been administered or controlled by the Indians themselves and had been providing them with an opportunity to manage some of their own affairs. Secondly, in the case of programs to be transferred to the states, the step would be in the direction of termination, opening the door to further moves in the same dreaded direction. Indians knew from experience that their position would deteriorate if they had to deal with the states. On both counts, therefore, the proposed changes were moves away from self-determination and the kind of freedom the Indians had been seeking.

Among the Indian groups that protested this new development were the Eastern Cherokee of North Carolina, the Choctaw of Mississippi, and the

Florida Seminole and Miccosukee (a group that had broken away from the Seminole). Joined in an organization called the United Southeastern Tribes, these Indians were descendants of Southern Indians who, by going into hiding, had managed to evade the cruel removal of their fellow tribesmen from the southeastern states to Oklahoma by troops sent by Presidents Jackson and Van Buren in the 1830's. In time the Indians had come out of hiding, but they were unrecognized by the federal government and for the most part ignored by the states in which they dwelled. As their condition worsened in the twentieth century, the federal government finally took cognizance of their needs and established relations with them, providing protection and certain services to them.

Now, in the face of a threat to turn them back to the state governments, they reacted like Indians in all parts of the country. The following excerpts from a policy statement issued by them in the fall of 1969 reflect many concerns: the reorganization of the BIA, the proposals to turn programs over to the states and localities, the repositioning of the BIA or parts of that agency among other sections of the government, and the ending of the programs that they had managed for themselves. But in sum, it was again the voice of Indians pressing for self-determination.

Members of the United Southeastern Tribes (USET composed of the Eastern Band of Cherokee Indians, the Mississippi Band of Choctaw Indians, and the Seminole and Miccosukee Tribes of Florida) recognize the Federal Government as a long standing associate on Indian Reservations. Historically, the relationship between Indians and the Federal Government has been *defined* by the Federal Government and *imposed* upon Indian people. Changes in Indian programs have not been open to discussion by Indian people or their leaders until they have been analyzed politically by the Federal Government. In the most recent past, Indians have experienced more involvement in making decisions which affect them and thus have made some progress in influencing the policies of the dominant Federal Government.

The Indian people believe that since the Federal Government has declared a special obligation to the Indian people, the role of the Indian and the role of the Federal Government toward each other should be mutually agreed upon. We believe that these roles should *not* be defined as a partnership, but rather that *the Indian be recognized as the controller of his own destiny both in terms of the direction he chooses and the method of moving in that direction.*

We further believe that the Federal Government should be recognized as being no more or less than a support service to this direction and movement.

For these reasons, USET together with other Indian groups has viewed with interest the efforts of the current administration to take a fresh approach to many of the problems facing the American people. We are particularly gratified to note that the basic philosophy of programs now under consideration includes the need for more local control and involvement, the need for more comprehensive and flexible funding arrangements, and permits the tailoring of programs to better respond to local needs. The Indian people have long advocated the inclusion of these features in programs designed for Indians. While many of the programs under current consideration, such as manpower training and welfare, are not specially designed to affect the Indian people than any other recent legislation, other proposals under consideration, such as reorganization of the Bureau of Indian Affairs, affect Indian people directly.

Since these programs will have an impact on our people for years to come, we are profoundly concerned that in certain aspects they may represent a reversal of the previous trend toward greater Indian involvement in Indian affairs. We strongly oppose any reorganization of federal Indian programs which would fail to take into account the special relationship between the Federal Government and tribal Indians, the special responsibilities of the Federal Government with respect to Indian Tribes, and the right to be Indian, which is cherished by Indian people throughout America. We fear that well-meaning bureaucrats, who may want to help us, but who are not informed about reservation life or Indian thinking, may try to revert back to the old idea that the Government can turn an Indian into a white man by cutting off his braids.

In particular, the President's proposal to allow state and

158

local governments to assume a greater portion of the role in decision making in all aspects of Federal programs, i.e., welfare, manpower training, operation of the Office of Economic Opportunity and the tax sharing proposal, is potentially threatening to the well being of Indian people. We feel that in the attempt to decentralize power, the President assumes that by assigning administrative responsibility to the States and localities, control will be delegated to officials in touch with community needs. (Manpower Training Statement, August 12, 1969) We question whether state and local officials in the Southeastern United States are in touch with the needs of Indian people.

Unlike Indian people in some parts of the United States, we have had a long history of dealing directly with the state governments. Following the removal of the bulk of the Indian people west of the Mississippi in the early nineteenth century, those Indian people remaining in the southeast remained for almost one hundred years under the sole control of local and state governments. The suffering of the Indian people during this time is a matter of historical record. Almost without exception, state and local governments failed to provide adequate education, health services, or even protection under the law.

Only in the twentieth century did the Federal Government recognize the destitute condition of the Indian people in the southeast and the almost total lack of any effort by state and local governments to alleviate this situation. Federal services to our people were gradually provided by the Bureau of Indian Affairs since this was the only way Indian people could begin to progress. Often this progress has not been as rapid as it should have been, but without direct federal assistance there would have been little or no progress. Progress has accelerated within recent years as Indians have been permitted to take a greater role in making decisions on programs which affect them. This has permitted Indian programs to be more responsive to Indian needs.

The concern of USET is that such Indian controls will be weakened by exchanging Federal assistance which has been increasingly responsive to Indian participation in decision making for state and local control which could end Indian participation and return our people to the domination of non-Indian local governments with which we are all too familiar. Most state and local governments in the southeast have little knowledge for or appreciation of the problems of their Indian citizens. In many areas Indian people are still denied the basic rights of all citizens. Yet it is these state and local governments that will exercise increasing control of Federal programs in the southeast if the federal role in Indian affairs is transferred to the states.

USET is fearful that if local and state governments are given control over Indian programs, the Indian people will experience a *curtailment* in existing programs rather than *expansion* which is so urgently needed. USET recognizes that historically the Federal Government has maintained a higher standard of service and commitment than some of the states may be willing or able to provide.

Indians have the same social and economic needs as other citizens of the country including:

1. Adequate protection under the law.

2. Safe, sanitary housing.

3. An expanding, practical economic development program.

4. Assistance in the preservation of natural resources.

5. Assistance in the development of adequate jobs and training programs.

6. Assistance in helping those persons who are not able to help themselves with economic, social, or emotional problems.

7. Adequate resources to develop and operate a sound educational program for Indian youth.

8. Adequate resources and services for better health, and

9. Adequate resources to develop managerial and leadership skills to carry on the necessary efforts which lead to self-determination.

Although Indians are making every effort to understand the attitudes and values of non-Indians, there are still characteristics which are singularly Indian, which Indians value. Indians feel they can best progress while protecting their values. Indians also feel that Federal recognition of these characteristics and values will be lost if the administration of services to them is not maintained separately. In order to be most effective, Indian programs must not be lost in the overpowering hodge-podge of other Federal commitments. USET is not in favor of changing any programs or agencies dealing with Indians unless there can be *conclusive* proof that such change will provide more effective working programs.

In order that this be assured, USET recommends that Indians be involved in the pre-planning of all new programs affecting them. In order for us to make concrete suggestions, we feel that the administration should "spell out" the details as to how the President's proposals would affect the status of existing Indian programs. . . .

In the past, changes in Indian programs often have not been open to discussion by Indian people or their leaders, but have been promulgated as the result of the application of pressure by non-Indian interests with axes to grind. The Federal Government has made serious legal and moral commitments through treaties and by statute to provide assistance in the self-development and self-determination of Indian people. As long as these special needs exist and inasmuch as the Federal Government has declared this special commitment to assist America's most impoverished minority, it is essential that existing programs should continue at *an accelerated rate* rather than be curtailed as may be the case under proposed legislation.

In summary, what we ask for Indian people is "self-development," with emphasis equally distributed between "self" and "development." We do not want development to be something which is done *to* us, but something done *by* us. We want our own goals, attitudes, and cherished beliefs to be expressed in the way in which we develop. Indeed, all Indian tribes are not alike, and some of our tribes may seek one form of development, while others seek another.

The point is that no program to assist Indian people will work if it ignores the reality of our Indian way of life. As minorities in the states which we inhabit (and which once belonged to us) we have reason to doubt that the non-Indian state governments will, in the foreseeable future, respect our right to be Indian.

On the other hand, we have reason to look to the Federal Government, despite the mistakes of the past, with hope because federal programs have often provided us with the helping hand which we need in self-development.

We know that the existing federal programs for Indian people are being reexamined. This is right, and these programs should be improved and made more effective, but we urge the Administration and the Congress to be mindful of the repeated past failures of the government policies which have ignored the separate culture and way of life which Indian people continue to cherish. We ask this not in any disloyal spirit. Indian-Americans have proved their patriotism to the United States in every one of our modern wars.

Rather, we want to make it plain that we wish to be the kind of Americans that we are, not some other kind of American. We wish to be Cherokee, Choctaw, Miccosukee, and Seminole, all Americans, but also Indians. We wish to be good Indians, but Indians. This is the spirit in which we ask for your support.

APPENDIX

BUREAU OF INDIAN AFFAIRS. Several suggestions regarding changes in the status of the BIA, such as the proposal to administratively move the educational responsibility of the BIA to HEW, are a cause of serious concern. Of course, the need for continued emphasis in improving educational programs for Indians is obvious to anyone familiar with reservation life. The average educational level in one of our member tribes is second grade. In another, in that portion of the tribe which is involved in the share-cropper economy (approximately half the tribe's members), the educational level is 1.5 years. The shortcomings of the presently underfinanced Indian education programs are many. . . .

Indian education in most areas means special education and therefore requires more highly qualified professionals;

this means more money. The present hiring practice in Indian education is controlled by Civil Service regulations which do not allow for Indian involvement. More effective programs for Indian people require that there be more Indian control of program policies and thus more Indian involvement.

Any change in BIA status should be based on how best to insure more Indian control and involvement. If federal programs for Indians are divided among differing agencies at differing governmental levels, effective Indian control will become more difficult. If it is advisable to transfer Indian education from BIA to HEW, might it not also simplify matters to transfer all BIA to HEW and reintegrate the Indian Health Program under one office? However, we must repeat that such administrative changes mean little or nothing if they are not undertaken to increase Indian participation and involvement in Indian programs, and to provide more effective and better funded programs.

We favor the formation of Indian school boards with adequate powers given to the board to control and govern the activities of Indian education regardless of whether it remains within the Bureau of Indian Affairs or is transferred to the Department of Health, Education and Welfare. The establishment of school boards at the local level should be planned and endorsed by the Indian people prior to the implementation.

WELFARE PROGRAM. We agreed with the broad philosophy of the President's message of August 11, 1969. USET Representatives are particularly pleased that benefits as outlined will be extended to the "working poor" into which category many Indians fall. However, we are concerned that a local interpretation of the work requirement could be prejudicial to Indian people. We wonder what safeguards could be incorporated to prevent persons from being exploited by people who pay less than the minimum wage. We further wonder if the requirement to accept non-local jobs could be interpreted to require forced relocation from their communities to distant urban jobs. Past relocation programs have proven that many Indian people, although possessing adequate job training, do not adjust well to an urban environment. To forceably relocate such individuals would not help the individual Indian family nor the city to which they were relocated, but it could lead to the destruction of Indian communities.

MANPOWER TRAINING PROGRAM. We are in agreement with the concept of a comprehensive Manpower Program and we can see the need for consolidating training programs in the Department of Labor. However, the Community Work and Training Program of the Office of Economic Opportunity has made a great contribution to Indian needs by funding individual community programs for Indian people operated under the control of Indian people to serve Indian needs. We hope that this type of specific programs for Indian needs under the direction of Indian people will not be lost in the consolidation of training programs. Uniformity of training and program consolidation should not prevent funding of programs designed for specific local needs under the direction of local Indian people.

OFFICE OF ECONOMIC OPPORTUNITY. USET representatives feel that the various programs of the OEO have within the past years provided the best example of flexible response to local problems under the leadership of local Indian people. We favor the transfer of OEO functions to other branches of government only when this will clearly result in improved services to local needs. As indicated in our basic letter, we fear that when services transferred from OEO to other branches of government are then placed under the control of state and local governments rather than the groups to be served, true local control will be lost, and Indian needs will be ignored.

U.S. PUBLIC HEALTH SERVICE. The one commonality regarding health services of members of the USET is the fact that the amount of service falls far short of their needs. Such a simple statement need not be defended further than a visit to the facilities available on each of the reservations. Numerous statistics have been quoted over and over again regarding the condition of Indian health throughout the country. In addition to inadequate services and facilities available to

Indians in the southeast, there is also the problem of prejudice in the use of public facilities off the reservation. Indian children are infested with intestinal parasites and chances are better than even that by the time an Indian has reached adulthood he will have been exposed to infectious hepatitis, tuberculosis and/or diabetes. Standard tests given by the BIA and research people from various agencies reflect low achievement for Indian students. One dominant theory is that this low achievement is directly related to poor health, inadequate diet, unsanitary living conditions, and inadequate medical services. In addition to physical health needs, the problem of mental health is equally pressing, especially as it is reflected in the high rate of alcoholism. The closest mental health services provided by the U.S. Public Health Service exist in the person of one doctor located in Oklahoma City. Members of USET feel that along with other pressing needs, special efforts should be made to increase services of Public Health Services. It is unknown to members of USET whether such an appraisal of services has ever been done in the southeast. If such information has been gathered it is not known to Indian people.

The following list of ideas represents no more than a superficial appraisal of some conditions which should be corrected immediately.

1. Increase the staff of the service units to an adequate level. The current personnel levels are inadequate to care for acutely ill patients and for teaching preventative measures.

2. Increase the operating funds of our hospitals to an adequate level to allow more efficient use of our understaffed hospital personnel.

3. Replace the current dilapidated facilities, particularly the hospitals at Philadelphia, Mississippi and Cherokee, North Carolina.

4. Appropriate adequate funds to purchase new equipment to replace the worn out, obsolete and inadequate equipment.

5. Increase contract medical care funds so that modern

medicine which is only available in large medical centers can be utilized.

6. Increase the Community Health Representative Program to an adequate level in order to increase tribal involvement in health problems.

7. Public Health Nursing Programs and Health Education Programs must be staffed and funded. In both programs, increased use of local personnel should be made and scholarships provided for their training.

8. Lift the current freeze on sanitation projects in order that each family residing on tribal lands may be provided with adequate sanitation, i.e., fresh hot and cold water under pressure, complete bathrooms, and kitchen facilities.

9. Adequate programs for dental health should be funded to provide care for adults as well as children.

Through our mutual discussions in USET and with other intertribal organizations, we have become more and more aware that Indians have many problems in common. Thus, we are especially concerned that at least the concept of the "Bureau of Indian Affairs," in whatever department the agency is located, should not be abandoned. There should be a Commissioner charged with the responsibility for effectively administering all specifically Indian programs, such as education, health, tribal operations, and land and economic development. These specifically Indian programs should not be parcelled out to different agencies where the importance of Indian needs will be lost in the bureaucratic shuffle. Of course, we must take advantage of other governmental programs (OEO, EDA, and Manpower programs) but we know from experience that we need a highly ranked man in the Federal Administration whose job it is to look out for us as Indians.

In any review of ways to improve Indian programs, we respectfully request that our views should be considered.

INDIAN EDUCATION: A NATIONAL TRAGEDY AND CHALLENGE

1969 Report of the U.S. Senate Committee
on Labor and Public Welfare,
Made by its Special Subcommittee
on Indian Education

Historically, the federal government has assumed the responsibility for the education of Indian youths. Through the years the Bureau of Indian Affairs developed its own educational system, which has included both day and boarding schools, principally on, or adjacent to, reservations. As one of the only school systems run by the United States (another is administered by the Department of Defense for dependents of military personnel overseas), it might be expected to be a model of excellence. Instead, both Indians and non-Indians have attacked it for years as a national scandal—ill-equipped and maladministered, unresponsive to Indian backgrounds and needs, and positively injurious to the mental health and future of its students.

During the 1960's increasing attention was paid to the deficiencies of Indian education. With good cause, Indian self-determinists began to demand that tribes take full control of the BIA schools that their children attended. For one thing, they felt acutely the harmful effects of a white man's school system, which in trying to turn Indian children into whites as fast as possible, taught them nothing about their own Indian heritage and culture, shamed them for their Indianness, and left them stranded, without pride or self-assurance, neither white nor Indian.

Before he left office, President Johnson recommended that the BIA encourage the formation of Indian school boards for all federal schools, but by 1969 little progress had been made in that direction, principally because of opposition by the Bureau of the Budget. Indians, supported by a growing number of professional educators, had meanwhile intensified their criticism, going beyond the idea of merely establishing Indian school boards to a position in which they viewed Indian control of the education of their youths as a necessary basis for Indian management and control of all their own affairs.

Much ammunition was provided critics of the existing system by the publication, in the fall of 1969, of the final report of a Special Senate Subcommittee on Indian Education. Under the chairmanship first of Senator Robert Kennedy and then, after his death, of his brother, Senator Edward Kennedy, the subcommittee had conducted a long and thorough examination of the subject. As might have been expected, the BIA, which was the principal target of the report, paid little attention to it, and nothing immediately resulted from its publication. But the facts, succinctly surveyed in the following summary that preceded the body of the report, provided powerful arguments for Indians who were fighting for control of their schools.

For more than two years the members of this subcommittee have been gauging how well American Indians are educated. We have traveled to all parts of the country; we have visited Indians in their homes and in their schools; we have listened to Indians, to Government officials, and to experts; and we have looked closely into every aspect of the educational opportunities this Nation offers its Indian citizens.

Our work fills 4,077 pages in seven volumes of hearings and 450 pages in five volumes of committee prints. This report is the distillate of this work.

We are shocked at what we discovered.

Others before us were shocked. They recommended and made changes. Others after us will likely be shocked, too—despite our recommendations and efforts at reform. For there is so much to do—wrongs to right, omissions to fill, untruths to correct—that our own recommendations, concerned as they are with education alone, need supplementation across the whole board of Indian life.

We have developed page after page of statistics. These cold figures mark a stain on our national conscience, a stain which has spread slowly for hundreds of years. They tell a story, to be sure. But they cannot tell the whole story. They cannot, for example, tell of the despair, the frustration, the hopelessness, the poignancy, of children who want to learn but are not taught; of adults who try to read but have no one to teach them; of families which want to stay together but are forced apart; or of 9-year-old children who want neighborhood schools but are sent thousands of miles away to remote and alien boarding schools.

We have seen what these conditions do to Indian children and Indian families. The sights are not pleasant.

We have concluded that our national policies for educating American Indians are a failure of major proportions. They have not offered Indian children—either in years past or to-day—an educational opportunity anywhere near equal to that offered the great bulk of American children. Past generations of lawmakers and administrators have failed the American Indian. Our own generation thus faces a challenge—we can continue the unacceptable policies and programs of the past or we can recognize our failures, renew our commitments, and reinvest our efforts with new energy.

It is this latter course that the subcommittee chooses. We have made 60 separate recommendations. If they are all carried into force and effect, then we believe that all American Indians, children and adults, will have the unfettered opportunity to grow to their full potential. Decent education has been denied Indians in the past, and they have fallen far short of matching their promise with performance. But this need not always be so. Creative, imaginative, and above all, relevant educational experiences can blot the stain on our national conscience. This is the challenge the subcommittee believes faces our own generation.

This Nation's 600,000 American Indians are a diverse ethnic group. They live in all 50 States and speak some 300 separate languages. Four hundred thousand Indians live on reservations, and 200,000 live off reservations. The tribes have different customs and mores, and different wants and needs. The urban Indian has a world different from that of the rural Indian.

Indian children attend Federal, public, private, and mission schools. In the early days of this republic, what little formal education there was available to Indians was under the control of the church. Gradually, however, as the Nation expanded westward and Indian nations were conquered, the treaties between the conquering United States and the defeated Indian nations provided for the establishment of schools for Indian children. In 1842, for example, there were 37 Indian schools run by the U.S. Government. This number had increased to 106 in 1881, and to 226 in 1968.

This pattern of Federal responsibility for Indian education has been slowly changing. In 1968, for example, the education of Indian children in California, Idaho, Michigan, Minnesota, Nebraska, Oregon, Texas, Washington, and Wisconsin was the total responsibility of the State and not the Federal Government.

In 1968 there were 152,088 Indian children between the ages of 6 and 18. 142,630 attended one type of school or another. Most of these—61.3 percent—attended public, non-Federal schools with non-Indian children. Another 32.7 percent were enrolled in Federal schools, and 6.0 percent attended mission and other schools. Some 6,616 school-age Indian children were not in school at all. The Bureau of Indian Affairs in the Department of the Interior, the Federal agency charged with managing Indian affairs for the United States, was unable to determine the educational status of some 2,842 Indian children.

The Bureau of Indian Affairs operates 77 boarding schools and 147 day schools. There are 35,309 school-age Indian children in these boarding schools, and 16,139 in the day schools. Nearly 9,000 of the boarding-school children are under 9 years old.

In its investigation of "any and all matters pertaining to the education of Indian children" (S. Res. 165, August 31, 1967), the subcommittee thus was compelled to examine not only the Federal schools, but the State and local public schools and the mission schools as well.

What concerned us most deeply, as we carried out our mandate, was the low quality of virtually every aspect of the schooling available to Indian children. The school buildings themselves; the course materials and books; the attitude of teachers and administrative personnel; the accessibility of school buildings—all these are of shocking quality.

A few of the statistics we developed:

Forty thousand Navajo Indians, nearly a third of the entire tribe, are functional illiterates in English;

The average educational level for all Indians under Federal supervision is 5 school years;

More than one out of every five Indian men have less than 5 years of schooling;

Dropout rates for Indians are twice the national average;

In New Mexico, some Indian high school students walk 2 miles to the bus every day and then ride 50 miles to school;

The average age of top level BIA education administrators is 58 years;

In 1953 the BIA began a crash program to improve education for Navajo children. Between then and 1967, supervisory positions in BIA headquarters increased 113 percent; supervisory positions in BIA schools increased 144 percent; administrative and clerical positions in the BIA schools increased 94 percent. Yet, teaching positions increased only 20 percent;

In one school in Oklahoma the student body is 100 percent Indian; yet it is controlled by a three-man, non-Indian school board.

Only 18 percent of the students in Federal Indian schools go on to college; the national average is 50 percent;

Only 3 percent of Indian students who enroll in college graduate; the national average is 32 percent;

The BIA spends only $18 per year per child on textbooks and supplies, compared to a national average of $40;

Only one of every 100 Indian college graduates will receive a masters degree; and

Despite a Presidential directive 2 years ago, only one of the 226 BIA schools is governed by an elective school board.

These are only a few of the statistics which tell the story of how poor the quality of education is that American Indians have available to them. Running all through this report are many others, which are some measure of the depth of the tragedy. There are, too, specific examples of visits we made to various facilities in the Indian education system. These are too lengthy to summarize; however, the subcommittee believes that their cumulative effect is chilling.

We reacted to our findings by making a long series of specific recommendations. These recommendations embrace legislative changes; administrative changes; policy changes; structural changes—all of which are geared to making Indian education programs into models of excellence, not of bureaucratic calcification.

We have recommended that the Nation adopt as national policy a commitment to achieving educational excellence for American Indians. We have recommended that the Nation adopt as national goals a series of specific objectives relating to educational opportunities for American Indians. Taken together, this policy and these goals are a framework for a program of action. Clearly, this action program needs legislative and executive support if it is to meet its promise. Most of all, however, it needs dedicated and imaginative management by those Federal officials, and State and local officials as well, who have the principal responsibilities for educating American Indians.

We have recommended that there be convened a White House Conference on American Indian Affairs. We have recommended—although not unanimously—that there be established a Senate Select Committee on the Human Needs of American Indians. We have recommended the enactment of a comprehensive Indian education statute, to replace the fragmented and inadequate education legislation now extant. We have recommended that the funds available for Indian education programs be markedly increased.

One theme running through all our recommendations is increased Indian participation and control of their own education programs. For far too long, the Nation has paid only token heed to the notion that Indians should have a strong voice in their own destiny. We have made a number of recommendations to correct this historic, anomalous paternalism. We have, for example, recommended that the Commissioner of the BIA be raised to the level of Assistant Secretary of the Department of Interior; that there be established a National Indian Board of Indian Education with authority to set standards and criteria for the Federal Indian schools; that local Indian boards of education be established for Indian school districts; and that Indian parental and community involvement be increased. These reforms, taken together, can—at last—make education of American Indians relevant to the lives of American Indians.

We have recommended programs to meet special, unmet needs in the Indian education field. Culturally-sensitive curriculum materials, for example, are seriously lacking; so are bi-lingual education efforts. Little educational material is available to Indians concerning nutrition and alcoholism. We have developed proposals in all these fields, and made strong recommendations to rectify their presently unacceptable status.

The subcommittee spent much time and devoted considerable effort to the "organization problem," a problem of long and high concern to those seeking reform of our policies toward American Indians. It is, in fact, two problems bound up as one—the internal organization of the Bureau of Indian Affairs, and the location of the Bureau within the Federal establishment. We made no final recommendation on this most serious issue. Instead, because we believe it critically important that the Indians themselves express their voices on this matter, we have suggested that it be put high on the agenda of the White House Conference on American Indian Affairs. Because, as we conceive it, this White House Conference will be organized by the Indians themselves, with the support of the National Council on Indian Opportunity, it is entirely appropriate that this organization problem be left for the conference.

In this report, we have compared the size and scope of the effort we believe must be mounted to the Marshall Plan which revitalized postwar Europe. We believe that we have, as a Nation, as great a moral and legal obligation to our Indian citizens today as we did after World War II to our European allies and adversaries.

The scope of this subcommittee's work was limited by its authorizing resolution to education. But as we traveled, and listened, and saw, we learned that education cannot be isolated from the other aspects of Indian life. These aspects, too, have much room for improvement. This lies in part behind the recommendation for a Senate Select Committee on the Human Needs of American Indians. Economic development, job training, legal representation in water rights and oil lease matters—these are only a few of the correlative problems sorely in need of attention.

In conclusion, it is sufficient to restate our basic finding: that our Nation's policies and programs for educating American Indians are a national tragedy. They present us with a national challenge of no small proportions. We believe that this report recommends the proper steps to meet this challenge. But we know that it will not be met without strong leadership and dedicated work. We believe that with this leadership for the Congress and the executive branch of the Government, the Nation can and will meet this challenge.

INDIAN EDUCATION: A CHALLENGE FOR THE CHURCH

by Helen M. Scheirbeck

The White House Conference on Indian Affairs, recommended by the Senate Subcommittee on Indian Education, was not held. But the subcommittee's report helped to further Indian sentiment for assuming control of their children's education.

Showing the way to other tribes, the Navajo had established the Rough Rock Demonstration School—bringing Navajo children and adults together in an innovative learning process based in great part on Navajo culture—and the Navajo Community College, the first institution of higher learning run by Indians for Indians. Soon other tribes began to seek the means of running their own schools, negotiating for the assumption of control of various units in the BIA system as well as certain state public schools in which the majority of the pupils were Indian. The process was not to be effected overnight. There were many problems, not least of which were the Indians' needs for funding for their schools, and for the white man to keep hands off and allow the tribes to achieve true control.

Among persuasive Indian statements on the subject was the following address in 1970 by Helen M. Scheirbeck, a Lumbee Indian from North Carolina and at the time Director of Indian Education for the Department of Health, Education and Welfare, a job that included overseeing Indian participation in educational programs of that department. Although Miss Scheirbeck was speaking to a gathering of church representatives interested in Indian welfare, her remarks could have been made to any non-Indian audience.

In Busby, Montana, a first-grade teacher says, "The problem with Indians is that they hate themselves. As long as they are full of hate, they will not be able to learn to live in our society."

In New Mexico, a state official remarks, "You know what they're teaching those Indians out at Navajo Community College? They're teaching them that Geronimo and Sitting Bull and all those other clowns were duped by the white man. When are they going to start teaching the truth?"

In Washington, an Office of Education senior staff member refers in conversation to "my Indians" and "their problems."

The basic problem of the American Indian is the American white man. In education as in all things, years of racism, some conscious, some unconscious, have kept Indian education a fashionable pastime for "concerned" whites, as long as American Indians were not loud or ungrateful for pittances tossed their way. At the root of all Indian problems today lies the callous indifference or malicious interference of white men, bent on economic or political gain. In education as in all areas, one has to deal first with this issue, and second with actual program commitments to various Indian groups.

A recent Mauldin cartoon portrayed an Indian leaning over a reservation fence, suggesting to a black that "there's no neglect like 'benign neglect.'" This explains part of the national response to aboriginal Americans. Somehow even today we allow incredible poverty and disease to afflict so many of our citizens, with American Indians accounting for more than their proportionate share. Let me add some of the facts about American Indians in this country today.

680,000 live in the United States, including Alaska. 240,000 Indian children are of school age (5–17) according to the Bureau of Indian Affairs.

As a general educational characteristic, the adult Indian population has a much lower level of formal schooling than do other groups, and data on Indian young people reflect lower participation in formal education than other groups.

To be more specific, two out of every three Indian adults (25 years old and over) had no education beyond the elementary school grades and only one in four had more than five years of formal school. These people would be regarded as functional illiterates as far as the White educational system is concerned.

Rather than bore you with dropout and lack of retention statistics, I will quote from former Commissioner of Indian

Affairs, Philleo Nash, who has said, "The familiar, and by now dreary statistic was again produced, Indian children in public schools achieve at a higher level, age-for-age, than do Indian children in Federal schools. Of the over-all conclusions, only one new item stands forth . . . Indian children fall progressively behind their white counterparts, age-for-age, as they move through the graded school system."

The Federal educational policy for Indians has been clearly to put them in vocational areas, not in the academic or professional careers. Over the years, the formal education of American Indians has been the responsibility of three major groups — Christian missionaries, the Federal government, and the state public school system.

Mission schools were the major way for educating American Indians until the last part of the 19th century. After the Civil War, the Federal boarding schools became the important educational method. Today the state public schools educate over half of all Indian children for which the Federal government assumes responsibility.

With the benevolent interest of the church, the states, and the Federal government in Indian education, why is the topic Indian education on your agenda this evening?

American Indians right now are struggling as never before, to develop their communities, their institutions, and their leaders and [to] assume their rightful place as Indians in our society. This sounds most peculiar, because we are describing the struggle of people, "who were here first," who welcomed your ancestors and provided them with food, and who moved over willingly at first, and then with violent reluctance, to give to everyone a homeland.

Education for so long to the Indian has been the way to become white. Only in the last decade are Indians beginning to see education as a tool to help them preserve their own communities and develop their own life styles according to their own standards.

Indian people must have control over their schools, from hiring the teachers and administrators, to operating the schools. These schools must be in their communities. Career horizons must be expanded so that young Indians can pursue their interests whether they be the highly specialized skills of doctors and lawyers, or those of a garage mechanic. The freedom to explore all areas of career development must be made available to Indian people.

The crux of the educational problems for American Indians is largely one of control. Programs which affect the lives of Indians rarely are conceived, planned, funded, operated or controlled by Indians.

If the National Council of Churches and churches individually can honestly understand and deal with the need to involve Indians, not only in planning and operation, but specifically in the monetary and policy-making control of the venture, then they will indeed be rendering a worthwhile service to the Indian community. If the church is unable to relinquish control, they can best serve American Indians by not meddling in local affairs.

American Indians are not now, have never been, and never will be blind to what is going on around them. They know what they want, and increasingly they are going out and getting it. In education particularly, they are taking control of school systems, establishing private secondary and post-secondary institutions to provide an alternative to a white culture they do not entirely want. But they do need help, on their terms. Some of the areas in which church involvement can be helpful are in reading programs at the elementary level, college and career counselling, community education programs, teacher preparation, curriculum development and material resources.

Pre-school reading programs, undertaken with the support of the tribal council, can help Indian children (particularly those who speak an Indian tongue at home) get a head start on formal education. An appreciation for reading, familiarity with books, and mastery of basic skills are building blocks for later life experiences and are a major determinant of access to higher education. A number of programs already exist, and some are targeted for certain Indian children. What is never planned, however, is the role of the "instructor." Far too often well-meaning but insensitive volunteers or church people expect Indian youngsters to behave according to certain cultural norms (white norms), and as a result of the Indian children's "failure" to do so, they become exasperated and frustrated—a situation which offers little potential for success. Careful training of the personnel is such a fundamental issue that it can not be stressed too much, but it is almost always underplayed or ignored altogether.

Counselling programs for high school age youth are badly needed. Most BIA or local school counsellors offer little encouragement and even less practical advice to Indian young people. Carefully trained people could step in and supply these students with solid advice and assistance. Note carefully the first three words of that last sentence. If you do not know what they mean, don't send anyone at all.

Community education is an evolving concept in this country, and Indian communities are expressing interest in its potential. What is needed is a team of renaissance men and women to help define and subsequently serve the educational needs of a given community, from cradle to grave. The church would seem ideal to serve this purpose, since it could use facilities in the local community and provide extension service as well. Curriculum would, as implied earlier, spring from perceived needs of people, not from an Office in Washington, New York, or Chicago. And as long as the service is free, its success can be measured by Indian participation and feedback.

Church involvement in preparation of teachers who work with Indian children is another area where much needs to be done. When BIA schools experience 90% turnover from one year to the next, it follows that more training and exposure to indigenous Indian life could help better prepare those about to work with Indian children. Renewal experiences in mid-career would certainly represent an attempt to stimulate changes in teachers as well. The church could serve to improve the quality of available manpower. It might begin by assisting Indian young people seeking careers in education. While an influx of Indian teachers into mission, BIA and public schools is no guarantee that over-all educational improvement of Indian children will result, it is a certainty that their absence has substantially contributed to the belief by many Indian young people that the white man's education is of little value or relevance to himself or his people.

Closely parallel to teacher improvement is the need for curriculum development, and here again there is a substantial role for church energy and money. Elementary readers rarely depict any skin color other than white—we do not have to belabor the Coleman Report's findings on self-concept to know what has to be done. But as Indian young people grow older, and move into high school and college, they continue to encounter curricula designed for and by white middle class society. Imagine what your interest would be if, on the one hand, you could look out the window and see the vitality of a bustling city; if you made constant use of its technology (TV, radio, subway, bus, electricity, cinema, escalator, elevator, etc.), your orientation would quite properly be a technological one. What value would you then place on a curriculum which in large measure was oriented to an agrarian economy, with totally different family patterns, and a curriculum which continually ignored the city and its inhabitants in favor of small, rural community life? After years of subtle value judgments assuring you that the rustic and rural environment was more important than the urban and technological, you would be at best confused by this apparent contradiction. Your own experience would demonstrate to you the value of city life, while in school each day, teachers (most with rural backgrounds and value systems) would extol the virtues of country life. Reverse the roles and the clear and shocking failure of the "typical" Indian curriculum is clearly apparent—a failure that reflects unfavorably on both life styles and leaves the student with a severe social and educational trauma.

In many schools where Indian children are enrolled, insufficient supplies and materials plague the operation of the school program. Simple things such as paper clips and chalk are needed, and major investments, such as video recorders, movie projectors, and sports equipment, are usually at a premium. The church could wisely invest dollars in better supplying those engaged in the education of Indian young people, which would be a minimal investment with far-reaching benefits.

Before turning to specific National Council of Churches recommendations, I would like to discuss with you briefly another area which affects the education of Indian people, the life patterns in dormitories at boarding schools. If you have not yet visited an Indian boarding school, and talked freely and frankly with these students about regulations, inhumanity, pettiness, and general insensitivity to their growth needs (all of which help to condition their attitudes toward learning), I ask you to do so. The suffering is incalculable and the waste in human spirit is tragic. The list is long of repressive tactics employed against students by "qualified" officials of these dormitory complexes. We also know from talking with these young people that a type of psychological subjugation has been used to preclude such activities as questioning the actions of any authority figure. Most dormitories are in poor condition. The church can and should examine its own dormitories first, and offer them as models which the BIA could emulate. The key to success in this effort is an honest quest for Indian involvement in the administration of these dormitories, by both students and parents, and the rigorous recruiting of qualified and concerned personnel. Reform will not come about through either ignorance or apathy of these tragic conditions.

The Indian community does not need more task forces. It does not need more studies. It does not need more fact-finding tours or conferences to see what is wrong. What the American Indian desperately needs is a personal and organizational commitment, in personnel, money, and effort. . . .

INDIAN IDENTITY AND ECONOMIC DEVELOPMENT

by Sol Tax and Sam Stanley

January 18, 1970, saw the publication of another important Senate document on Indian affairs—a compendium of papers on different aspects of Indian economic development submitted by a number of authoritative writers to Senator William Proxmire of Wisconsin, chairman of the Subcommittee on Economy in Government of the Joint Economic Committee of Congress, and published by the committee under the title *Toward Economic Development for Native American Communities*. The papers examined many of the basic and most serious problems faced by the tribes as they struggled to take control of their own affairs and create better lives for their people.

A particular value of many of the papers was the insights and perspectives they gave non-Indians in and out of government on the difficulties and obstacles that white men were placing in the way of Indian development. The identification to the non-Indian of these hobbling and destructive roadblocks was a necessary first step if the white man himself was to acknowledge his injustices and erroneous thinking, support the Indians in bringing them to an end, and permit the tribes to move ahead.

A fundamental consideration—the recognition of what might be termed the Indian's point of view—was the substance of one paper, "Indian Identity and Economic Development," by Dr. Sol Tax, professor of anthropology at the University of Chicago and acting director of the Smithsonian Institution's Center for the Study of Man, and Dr. Sam Stanley, program coordinator for the center. Arguing that an understanding of the type of economic development desired by the Indians was basic to the success of any program, the authors went on to suggest that the Indians had two simultaneous goals: the protection of their cultural identity and an adequate economic adjustment to the modern environment. When, in the past, they were free to do so, Indians adapted successfully to changing environments. But they cannot be *forced* to make adjustments. Instead, the road to development lies in giving Indian groups maximum autonomy and the right to manage their own funds. In other words, as the following excerpts make clear, self-determination is required for successful Indian economic development.

It is "unnatural," perhaps impossible, for Indians to be isolated from their communities. Traditionally, the communities banded into larger political units called "tribes" or nations, which were recognized by European nations as sovereign. But the smaller communities, whether "sovereign" or not, were indispensable and valid units.

These "communities," recognized by their Indian members, must also be recognized as the units with which governmental Indian policy must deal. Individual families and persons have rights guaranteed to every citizen, and legislation need not concern them. Indian *communities* are recipients of what special rights, tradition, treaties and the needs of Indians require.

Legislation for American Indians has in the past been unsuccessful both because communities have been forced to operate in terms of our culture rather than their own and because they had no ultimate authority over internal management, being subject to veto power—hence constant surveillance—from outside. What is required, therefore, is a legislative program which provides maximum internal autonomy and authority for Indian communities.

American Indian communities require funds for education, health, welfare and economic development. The general society provides such funds to replace the resource base which —if restored—would provide independence. Since the resource base (the continent which Europeans occupied) cannot be restored to Indian communities, money must be substituted. Just as Indian communities managed their resources independently before, for the money to be useful they must manage it independently now.

The legislation required must, therefore, be drafted in such a way that each of the many hundreds of American Indian communities, however they are defined and bounded by Indians—from the small bands and subtribes to recreated urban "Indian center" communities—can each in its own way autonomously manage the resources that must be provided.

It would be indeed a strange procedure to try to draft such

legislation without full participation of the Indian communities. What is clearly required is Indian-community self-determination for developing the conditions of their self-determination. . . .

Through all of our history, States as well as the Federal Government have been frustrated with respect to solving the problems of the American Indians.

We have vacillated between (1) a policy of starving the Indians into throwing in the sponge and "getting lost" in the general population, and (2) a kinder policy of helping them to get themselves ready to leave Indian ways and get lost in the general population. In either case, they would then be off our consciences, and finally out of our pocketbooks. Both policies have failed.

When we have followed the first policy, and thrown them into the water to "sink or swim," we have found that the Indians neither sink nor swim; they just float, and remain the same problem. When we have followed the second, kinder policy, we have found that Indians do not, in fact, do the things that will lead to their disappearance. They do not want to get lost.

The "kind" policy will work only if we have the patience to continue to use our resources to help Indian communities to adjust to the national economy freely and in their own way. But their own way might not be to get lost at all.

Every man and woman has the personal problem of deciding what sort of person he wants to be. Some Indians may want to become white men in their allegiance and their ways; this ought to be their right. But many Indians want to maintain their Indian values and allegiance, and many Indian communities want to maintain for their posterity an identity and heritage that were given to them. They too have this right.

It is not for any white man, or Congress or the Indian Service bureaucracy, to demand that Indians stop being Indians.

It is a challenge which has never been met in the United States to help the Indians to adjust economically and socially to American life so that they actually become financially independent. We cannot begin to solve the problem unless we

185

first recognize that Indians have a right to make this adjustment *as* Indians.

Leaving them free to make their own choices removes the great block to constructive change. What folly it has been to demand that Indians cooperate in plans for making them something other than they want to be! What an interesting experiment, on the other hand, once the block is removed, to develop with them ways toward that greatest freedom which comes with economic independence!

The Indian policy that has most recently been with us has been the sink or swim policy, the less moral way that has never worked and never can. It does not get Indians out of our pocketbooks—indeed, this un-Christian policy (as Gen. Eisenhower once called it) requires more money rather than less—and it certainly does not get them off the conscience of the nation.

The present policy, aimed at the disappearance of the Indians, is a double-edged sword. On the one side, there is a nauseating paternalism. Indians get help from the government because, since we destroyed their means of livelihood, they need it, and it is our moral obligation to continue this help until we and they are wise enough to make them once again independent. But meanwhile the Indian Bureau, like any overprotective parent, demands that the Indians manage their own affairs; but, on the grounds that they do not know how, never lets them try, and becomes sure, more than ever, that they are incompetent to do so.

They say, in effect, that as long as we pay the bills, we shall manage your communities. If you think you are competent to manage your own affairs, then cut yourselves off from the financial assistance as well. Money to live on, or freedom; you can't have both, so take your choice.

But the Indians have not the resources for the medical, educational and developmental needs of their communities. So they must choose the continued interference in their local affairs. This satisfies nobody and gets nowhere. Congress, frustrated, then attempts to use force or bribery to induce Indian communities to make the other choice.

We need an entirely new approach. We need to separate the two problems *of the money which the Indians need for their community services* from *the way the money is used.*

Nobody should ever again interpret our policy as one which is importantly influenced by a desire to save money to the detriment of Indians and in violation of our traditional and moral obligations. It has been and should be our policy to *make it unnecessary to provide special services,* hence to make Indians independent. But until this is accomplished, the money should be provided because it is needed and because it is right.

Therefore, the first plank of our policy is to assure Indians that we shall continue to provide in the federal budget the money needed to continue Indian services. For the time being, we suggest that the same budget now provided be continued.

But this money should be spent by the Indians, for themselves, rather than *for* the Indians by bureaucrats. Just as a government might provide a subsidy to a hospital or a university without taking over the functions of administering the hospital or university, so the funds available to Indians should be looked upon as subsidies to assist them to provide their own community services — health, welfare, public order, education, development.

But whatever changes occur from one system of administration to another or from one allocation to another, they should be entirely voluntary on the part of the Indians who are now recipients of the services for which the funds are provided. If Indians prefer to have the federal government agencies continue to administer their services, no change need be made. Whenever, however, an Indian community, or the recipients of services, wish to seek changes in administration, these changes should be provided at once. . . .

Funds for services should be continued for the same services. Funds for administration should be made flexible so that as much as necessary can be used by tribes with which to hire non-governmental help for administration of their affairs, when they wish to make a change; and to pay the expenses of a panel of volunteer advisers set up independent of the Department of Interior from which Indian communities may obtain general advice in planning changes in how their affairs may be administered.

If the Bureau of Indian Affairs withers away, it will be because Indians will find other ways, which they prefer, to have their funds administered. There will be no "termination" with respect to provision of services as long as they are needed by Indians. "Withdrawal" will occur not as the government withdraws from its obligations, but as the Indians withdraw from government interference in the administration of their services.

INDIAN WATER RIGHTS AND RESERVATION DEVELOPMENT

by William H. Veeder

Another contribution to the compendium of papers on Indian economic development published in January, 1970, by the Joint Economic Committee of Congress was unusually significant. Like other papers in the collection, "Federal Encroachment on Indian Water Rights and the Impairment of Reservation Development" underscored the point that as long as injustices continue to deny to Indians a basis on which to create a viable economy on their own terms, the so-called Indian problems will continue. But its author, William H. Veeder, Water Conservation and Utilization Specialist in the Bureau of Indian Affairs, was the nation's top recognized authority on Indian water rights—a subject of life-and-death importance to most Western tribes—and his paper struck squarely and with telling precision at one of the key problems in federal-Indian relations: the conflict of interest within the Interior and Justice departments between the rights of Indians and the competing interests of non-Indians who are represented by various agencies of Interior.

The February, 1969, report to President Nixon, as well as other studies, had called attention to the way in which this conflict within the federal government victimized the Indians. But Veeder's paper, outlining in detail numerous examples of conflicts of interest within the Interior and Justice departments that prevented the Indians from receiving protections guaranteed to them, showed vividly the devastating consequences that Indian tribes had suffered. "Water is to the land what blood is to the body," Indians have said. The full significance of Veeder's paper was that it made clear that without the protection of the Indians' resources—in this case, water—few, if any, problems of a reservation could be solved. Indian survival, in fact, would be at stake.

Following is the summary that preceded Veeder's in-depth study. The recommendation at the end was later adopted in principle by President Nixon and presented to Congress as a piece of proposed legislation in the summer of 1970.

1. American Indian Reservations in the western United States contain invaluable natural resources. These include the land of which they are comprised, minerals, forests, lakes, streams and other sources of water which arise upon, border, traverse or underlie the Reservations.

2. Economic development of the western Reservations is inseparable from Indian rights to the use of water, which in turn is the most valuable of all natural resources in the arid and semiarid regions. Those rights are the catalyst for all economic development. Without them the Reservations are virtually uninhabitable, the soil remains untilled, the minerals remain in place, and poverty is pervasive.

3. Since time immemorial the Indians' water resources were inextricably a part of their way of life; indeed, a prime feature of their sustenance. Highly sophisticated irrigation systems were developed along the Gila River by the Pimas and Maricopas. Menominees harvested their wild rice, used the streams for travel, fishing and hunting. The Mohaves, Quechans and other Colorado River Indians depended on the stream's annual Nile-like floods to irrigate their crops. The Yakimas lived upon and traded salmon taken from the Columbia, as did the Northern Paiutes—the fish-eaters—who took the famous Lahonton cutthroat trout from the Truckee River and Pyramid Lake—their species destroyed by the Bureau of Reclamation.

4. The Indian *Winters Doctrine Rights* to the use of water in the streams or lakes which arise upon, border, traverse or underlie their Reservations, have been accorded by the Supreme Court and other courts a prior, paramount and superior status on the streams for the present and future economic development of the Western Reservations.

5. By the Constitution of the United States there was created a relationship between the Nation and the American Indians of transcendent dignity. That relationship of great dignity had its genesis in the policies adhered to by the European sovereigns who colonized this Continent and it was firmly established during the harsh and bitter years of the

Revolutionary War and the years which were to ensue prior to and including the adoption of the Constitution.

6. It has been declared that the relationship existing between the American Indians and the Nation "resembles that of a ward to his guardian"—a trust relationship with all of the express and implied obligations stemming from it. Only the uninformed ascribe to that trust a demeaning connotation in regard to the American Indians.

7. Great stress must be applied to the nature of the Indian trust property, including Indian rights to the use of water.

   (a) It is *private property,* legal title to which is held by the United States in trust for the American Indians as beneficial holders of equitable title.

   (b) Indian property is *not public property* as is the other property of the Nation.

8. Plenary power and responsibility under the Commerce Clause of the Constitution reside with the Congress to effectuate the trust relationship between the United States and the American Indians.

9. Congress is likewise invested by the Constitution with plenary power over the "public lands," all other lands, all rights to the use of water, title to which resides in the Nation. These lands and rights to the use of water are to be administered for the Nation as a whole. It is imperative that the nature of the right, title, interests and obligations of the Nation in regard to these properties held in trust for the Nation as a whole be sharply distinguished from the lands and rights to the use of water of the American Indians.

10. Congress in the exercise of its plenary power over the Nation's lands and rights to the use of water has invested the Department of the Interior with broad authority to administer, develop, sell, dispose of, and otherwise to take all required action respecting those lands and rights to the use of water. Agencies within the Department of the Interior carrying out the will of Congress in regard to those properties held for the public as a whole include but are not limited to: The Bureau of Reclamation, Bureau of Land Management, National Park

Service, Bureau of Outdoor Recreation and the agencies generally responsible for the propagation and protection of fish and wildlife.

11. Administrators, engineers, scientists, within the Department of the Interior, all acting within the scope of the authority vested in the Secretary of the Interior, are:

(1) Charged with the responsibility of fulfilling the Nation's trust status in regard to the Indian lands and rights to the use of water, which, as stated, are private in character, to be administered solely for the benefit of the Indians;

(2) Charged with the responsibility of administering lands and rights to the use of water claimed in connection with reclamation projects, administration of grazing districts, and other land uses requiring the exercise of rights to the use of water; fish and wildlife projects, recreational areas and other activities, all of which require rights in the streams.

12. (a) Lawyers in the Department of the Interior directly responsible to the Solicitor, in whom resides the obligation of performing the "legal" work for that Department; all of the agencies of it, including the Bureau of Indian Affairs, Indians and Indian Tribes, are constantly confronted with the sharp conflicts of interests between the Indian land and rights to the use of water, and the numerous other agencies referred to that likewise make claims to those waters and contest the rights and claims of the Indians to them;

(b) Lawyers in the Department of Justice directly responsible to the Attorney General, the Nation's chief law officer, have the responsibility:

(1) To defend, protect, preserve and have adjudicated, title to the lands of the Indians and their rights to the use of water, and otherwise to act as lawyers for the trustee obligated to perform with the fullest degree of loyalty to the Indians;

(2) To proceed as an adversary against the Indian claims for the seizure of their lands and rights to the use

of water, seeking to limit or otherwise defeat the claims of the Indians predicated upon the laws which other attorneys of the Justice Department are required effectively to espouse and advocate on behalf of the Indians;

(3) To perform legal services in regard to lands and rights to the use of water in streams and other water sources where the Indian rights are in conflict with claims of other agencies of the United States.

13. Both the administrators of the Department of the Interior and the lawyers of both Interior and Justice owe the highest degree of ethical, moral, loyal and equitable performance of their trust obligations to the American Indians. They are charged, moreover—as professionals—with the highest degree of care, skill and diligence in executing their broad assignments for the protection, preservation, administration and legal duties respecting Indian trust properties including, but not limited to, the invaluable Indian *Winters Doctrine Rights* to the use of water.

14. Conflicting responsibilities, obligations, interests, claims, legal theories—indeed, philosophies—oftentimes prevent the Interior and Justice Department administrators, planners, engineers and lawyers from fulfilling the trust obligation [which the Nation owes] to the American Indians in regard to natural resources, particularly in the complex and contentious field of Indian rights to the use of water in the arid and semiarid regions of western United States. Failure by those Departments, agencies and personnel to fulfill the Nation's obligation to protect and preserve Indian rights to the use of water includes, but most assuredly is not limited to: (a) Lack of knowledge of the existence, or the nature, measure and extent of those rights to the use of both surface and ground waters—refusal to recognize Indian rights are private rights to be administered separate, apart and independent of the "public rights" of the Nation as a whole in identically the same manner as other private rights are protected and preserved; (b) Lack of timely action to preserve, protect, conserve and administer those rights; (c) Inability or reluctance at the

decisional level to insist upon recognition and preservation of Indian rights to the use of water when to do so would prevent the construction—and/or administration in the manner desired—of a reclamation or other project conflicting with the Indians for water, the· supply of which is insufficient; (d) Attempted subordination, relinquishment, or conveyance of Indian rights to the use of water which are in conflict with other claims, Federal, State or local; (e) Failure to assert rights, interests and priorities of the Indians on a stream or project when to do so would limit the interests of non-Indians; (f) Opening Reservations to· non-Indian occupancy with the seizure of Indian land and rights to the use of water, with or without the payment of just compensation; (g) The imposition of servitudes, easements, and illegal occupancy or use of Indian lands and rights to the use of water.

15. Economic development of the American Indian Reservations in western United States, due largely to conflicting interests within the Interior and Justice Departments, or vacillating policies—a natural consequence of conflicting interests, responsibilities, and obligations within the Federal Establishment—has been (a) prevented by the abridgment or loss of Indian rights to the use of water; (b) intentionally prevented in whole or in part, or deferred in whole or in part, by the refusal to permit development of Indian lands with rights to the use of water.

16. Irreparable damage to the American Indians in western United States has ensued by reason of the consequences flowing from the conflicts described above. The Indians have suffered from extreme poverty, with the attendant ills of malnutrition, high infant mortality rate, reduced life expectancy, disease, and the shattering loss of human dignity which stems from poverty and deprivation of the necessities of life.

CONCLUSION

Economic development of the American Indian Reservations in western United States will continue to be prevented or severely curtailed in the absence of drastic changes in the laws and policies which would eliminate conflicting rights, responsibilities and obligations which presently exist among the several agencies of the National Government, all as reviewed in the accompanying memorandum and the summary set forth above.

RECOMMENDATION

Congress should enact legislation which would place in an agency independent from the Department of the Interior and the Department of Justice the full responsibility for the protection, preservation, administration, development, adjudication, determination, and control, including but not limited to all legal services required in connection with them, of the lands and rights to the use of water of the American Indian Reservations in western United States.

In furtherance of economic development of the American Indian Reservations in western United States it is imperative that there be undertaken an inventory of all of the Indian rights to the use of water in the streams and other sources of water arising upon, bordering upon, traversing or underlying their lands. This inventory should be undertaken with the objective of ascertaining, to the extent possible, the existence, character and measure of the rights as they relate to the present and future development of the Reservations. It is equally important to determine the highest and best use which can be made of these invaluable rights to the use of water and to chronicle those rights as they relate to each water source, indicating the highest and best present use to which they may be applied. They should likewise be evaluated from the standpoint of their maximum potential in the future by reason of the fact that those rights must be exercised in perpetuity and in contemplation of the ever-changing environment of western United States with its increasing population and water demands.

"WE MUST HOLD ON TO THE OLD WAYS"

Indians of All Tribes
Alcatraz Island, December 16, 1969

The striving for self-determination, nurtured by a new pride in Indian identity and background and symbolized by the slogan "Red Power," enlisted no more dedicated partisans than those Indians who lived away from reservations—at universities and in urban centers of the United States. By the end of the 1960's several hundred thousand—perhaps more than half a million—Indians lived in Chicago, Minneapolis, Denver, Los Angeles, and other major cities. Many of them had been lured there by World War II defense jobs, others by Bureau of Indian Affairs postwar relocation programs, and still others had gotten there on their own.

Adjusting to the alien "mainstream" of white culture was difficult for large numbers of them, and their lives were filled with social and economic problems every bit as serious as those of the reservations. Far from home, also, the urban Indians were cut off from the federal services to which they were entitled on the reservation. In their loneliness they tended to find each other, even though they came from different tribes and different parts of the country, and grouping together in urban Indian centers, they found strength and sustenance in their Indianness.

Among the young city and university Indians particularly, loyalty to their individual tribes and to the Indian people in general began to blaze high during the 1960's. From that point, militant advocacy of Indian self-determination and bitter hostility toward the Bureau of Indian Affairs and all other white oppressors of the Indians were a short step. Indian protest songs, sung by Johnny Cash, a descendant of Cherokee, Floyd Westerman, a Sioux, and Buffy Sainte-Marie, a Cree, inspired them, as did the writings of the young Standing Rock Sioux, Vine Deloria, Jr. *(Custer Died for Your Sins)*, and the Red Power and Indian nationalist speeches of Clyde Warrior, Wallace "Mad Bear" Anderson, Hank Adams, Lehman Brightman, Tillie Walker, and other Indians.

At many colleges Indian students formed their own clubs, conducted seminars and conferences on Indian problems, pressured for the introduction of Indian studies, and talked of off-campus activism in behalf of all the Indian peoples. In the cities so-called urban Indians formed activist organizations of their own, such as the American Indian Movement (AIM), under the direction of Clyde Bellecourt and Dennis Banks in Minneapolis, and the United Native Americans, Inc., led by Lehman Brightman in San Francisco. Some of the groups, together with previously existing Indian centers in various cities, joined in a nationwide federation called American Indians United, whose first head was Jess Six Killer, an Indian member of the Chicago Police Department.

Within the national context of non-Indian activist activities, marked especially by youth and minority group demonstrations, it was inevitable that Indian acts of protest would soon occur also. Old and new grievances were focused upon: the indifference of the government to long-standing injustices being suffered by tribes; the continued deafness by official Washington to the demand for self-determination; "stacked cards" against the Pyramid Lake Paiutes' right to water, the Taos Pueblos' right to their sacred Blue Lake, the Puget Sound Indians' right to fish, the Alaskan natives' right to their lands; exploitation of Indians by white promoters and advertisers; discrimination against Indians by federal, state, and local agencies of government; and the initial "realignment" of the Bureau of Indian Affairs, which failed to get at the heart of problems. These and other grievances stirred anger among the steadily growing groups of activists.

Then on November 20, 1969, a landing party of seventy-eight Indians calling themselves Indians of All Tribes suddenly occupied Alcatraz Island, in San Francisco Bay, electrifying Indians all over the United States and Canada and giving new inspiration to the cause of Indian freedom. Alcatraz, taken originally from Indians, had been employed in recent times by the federal government as a prison site. But the prison had been closed, and save for the operation of a lighthouse, the government no longer had use for the island. The Indians, most of whom lived or attended colleges in the San Francisco Bay area, moved onto the island under an old law that permitted certain tribes to reclaim land taken from them by the federal government when the government no longer needed it. They proclaimed Alcatraz to be Indian Land, and, though suffering hardships because of lack of water, food, and electricity, set about making their stay permanent.

Most of the non-Indians of the nation gave them their sympathy and support, and the government, not wishing to provoke a confrontation, let them stay — though wondering how, eventually, to oust them. San Franciscans sent food, medical supplies, and other assistance; tourists ferried to the island to give words of encouragement; and enthusiastic Indians from reservations and other urban areas came to live there temporarily or permanently.

Typical of the reactions of non-Indian well-wishers were the following sentiments by the Chairman of the American Bar Association's Committee on the American Indian, Monroe E. Price, a professor of law at UCLA and Deputy Director of California Indian Legal Services: "The taking of Alcatraz may begin a new era of Pan-Indian awareness and activity. That hard and lonely settlement has been greeted not with tear gas but with a sense of hope and promise. The band of Indians on the prison island have formed a policy for themselves and by themselves. They are staking a claim for the restoration of a culture and a strength of community that should not be lost. The wager they are asking the country to make is a safe one: that they cannot be more wrong than the great white fathers of the past."

Alcatraz was self-determination brought about by the Indians themselves. A community of, by, and for Indians was created. But the occupation of the island and the establishment of a settlement were not ends in themselves. On December 16, 1969, the group on Alcatraz addressed a letter to all the Indians of North America, inviting them to send delegates to a meeting on the island the following week. The letter set forth their ultimate goal, the establishment of an Indian cultural and educational center on Alcatraz. Many Indians from across the United States and Canada responded, and some stayed on the island, adding to its population, which soon represented fifty tribes.

The letter sent by the Alcatraz Indians on December 16, announcing the reason for the occupation of the island and the goal of the occupiers, follows.

Dear Brothers and Sisters:

This is a call for a delegation from each Indian nation, tribe or band from throughout the United States, Canada, and Mexico to meet together on Alcatraz Island in San Francisco Bay, on December 23, 1969, for a meeting to be tentatively called the Confederation of American Indian Nations (CAIN)

On November 20, 1969, 78 Indian people, under the name "Indians of all Tribes," moved onto Alcatraz Island, a former Federal Prison. We began cleaning up the Island and are still in the process of organizing, setting up classes and trying to instill the old Indian ways into our young.

We moved onto Alcatraz Island because we feel that Indian people need a Cultural Center of their own. For several decades, Indian people have not had enough control of training their young people. And without a cultural center of their own, we are afraid that the old Indian ways may be lost. We believe that the only way to keep them alive is for Indian people to do it themselves.

While it was a small group which moved onto the island, we want all Indian people to join with us. More Indian people from throughout the country are coming to the island every day. We are issuing this call in an attempt to unify all our Indian Brothers behind a common cause.

We realize that there are more problems in Indian communities besides having our culture taken away. We have water problems, land problems, "social" problems, job opportunity problems, and many others.

And as Vice President Agnew said at the annual convention of the National Congress of American Indians in October of this year, now is the time for Indian leadership.

We realize too that we are not getting anywhere fast by working alone as individual tribes. If we can gather together as brothers and come to a common agreement, we feel that we can be much more effective, doing things for ourselves, instead of having someone else doing it, telling us what is good for us.

So we must start somewhere. We feel that if we are going to succeed, we must hold on to the old ways. *This is the first and most important reason we went to Alcatraz Island.*

We feel that the only reason Indian people have been able to hold on and survive through decades of persecution and cultural deprivation is that the Indian way of life is and has been strong enough to hold the people together.

We hope to reinforce the traditional Indian way of life by building a Cultural Center on Alcatraz Island. We hope to build a college, a religious and spiritual center, a museum, a center of ecology, and a training school.

We hope to have the Cultural Center controlled by Indians, with the delegates from each Indian nation and urban center present for the first meeting on December 23, and at future meetings of the governing body.

We are inviting all our brothers to join with us on December 23, if not in person, then in spirit.

We are still raising funds for Alcatraz. The "Alcatraz Relief Fund" is established with the Bank of California, Mission Branch, 3060 16th Street, San Francisco, California 94103, and we are asking that donations of money go to the bank directly.

Many Indian Centers and tribal groups from throughout the country have supported the people on Alcatraz by conducting benefits, funded drives, and so forth. We are deeply appreciative of all the help we have received, and hope that all Indian people and people of good will, will join us in this effort.

We are also asking for formal resolutions of support from each organized Indian tribe and urban center. We can have great power at the bargaining table if we can get the support and help of all Indian people.

We have made no attempts at starting a hard and fast formal organization. We have elected spokesmen because someone has had to be a spokesman. We feel that all Indian people should be present or represented at the outset of a formal national Indian organization.

We have also elected a Central Council to help organize the day-to-day operation of the Island. This organization is not a governing body, but an operational one.

We hope to see you on December 23rd.

Indians of All Tribes
Alcatraz Island

STATEMENT OF THE INDIAN MEMBERS OF THE NATIONAL COUNCIL ON INDIAN OPPORTUNITY

January 26, 1970

The National Council on Indian Opportunity, created by a Presidential Executive Order on March 6, 1968, and ratified by Congress two years later, was one response by the federal government to the Indians' rising demand to participate in the formulation of policies and programs for their reservations.

The council contained six Indian members (increased in 1970 to eight), selected by the President from different parts of the country because of "their leadership ability and because they can fully represent Indian people from all regions of this nation." The Vice President of the United States was named chairman of the council, whose other members were the secretaries of Interior; Labor; Commerce; Agriculture; Health, Education and Welfare; and Housing and Urban Development; and the director of the Office of Economic Opportunity. In 1970 the Attorney General was added to the group.

The concept of the group was that it would serve as something of an ombudsman or super-watchdog in federal-Indian relations. Specifically, its functions were to see that Indians received the maximum benefits of programs of the different departments of the government; to encourage coordination and cooperation among the government agencies in their relations with the Indians; to appraise the impact and progress of federal programs used by Indians; and to suggest ways to improve such programs. The council met only occasionally during a year, but between meetings a non-Indian executive director and a small staff of Indians and non-Indians carried out its functions.

Indians accepted the council with mixed feelings. Many of them regarded it as another government bureaucracy controlled by white officials and "rubber stamped" by its Indian members, who would be unable to accomplish anything significant. Others, particularly tribal representatives, who were used to traveling to Washington and getting nowhere at the Bureau of Indian Affairs, found the NCIO a new and more potent and helpful audience for their problems and grievances. Staff members of the council, which was part of the Office of the Vice President, seemed to understand and sympathize with the desire for self-determination that colored Indian opinion. More than that, they were in a position to bring persuasive influence to bear on the individual federal agencies, and most importantly—when the Nixon administration took office—they could help see that the new administration's Indian policy, which would be unveiled in July, 1970, would accurately reflect Indian thinking.

As a means toward that goal, the following statement, delivered by the Indian members to the Vice President and the Cabinet members at a meeting of the council in the White House on January 26, 1970, was a significant one. The Indians were impatient with the administration's lack of action and its delay in announcing an Indian policy. Going beyond generalities, their carefully worked out statement enumerated precise Indian needs, and recommendations for solutions. Once again it was the voice of Indians demonstrating their ability to know best what their peoples required, but this time it was communicated directly to the highest officials in the government.

The Indian members of the council who presented the statement were Roger Jourdain, chairman of the Red Lake Chippewa Tribal Council; William Hensley, an Eskimo and member of the Alaska State Legislature; Wendell Chino, chairman of the Mescalero Apache Tribal Council; Cato Valandra of the Rosebud Sioux Tribe of South Dakota; Mrs. LaDonna Harris, Comanche Indian of Oklahoma and wife of Senator Fred Harris of that state; and Raymond Nakai, chairman of the Navajo Tribal Council. In addition a second statement, which follows the first one below, was presented to the council by Nakai, detailing a specific, and somewhat different, focus of need for the Navajo, the largest tribe in the country.

The knowledgeability and realism of both statements had an impact on Vice President Spiro Agnew, and because of his interest, the documents played an influential role with those on the council and in the White House, the Interior Department, and elsewhere in the government who were preparing the Republican administration's Indian policy.

STATEMENT OF THE INDIAN MEMBERS

- In 1970, when men have landed on the moon, many American Indians still do not have adequate roads to the nearest market.

- In 1970, when almost every American baby can look forward to a life expectancy of 70 years, the Indian infant mortality rate is three times higher than the national average after the first month of life.
- In 1970, when personal income in America is at an unprecedented level, unemployment among American Indians runs as high as 60%.

These are reasons why the National Council on Indian Opportunity—the first agency of the Federal Government where Indian leaders sit as equals with members of the President's Cabinet in overseeing Federal Indian programs and in recommending Federal Indian policy—is of the most vital importance to Indians all across the Nation. Because the essential requirement of any Indian policy must be active and prior Indian consultation and input before major decisions are taken which affect Indian lives, Indian membership on the Council is not only of symbolic importance, but is insurance that such consultation will be sought.

We wonder if the Vice President and the Cabinet Officers fully appreciate the fact of their physical presence here today —the meaning that it has for Indian people? We realize that every group in America would like to have you arrayed before them, commanding your attention.

For the Indian people across the nation to know that at this moment the Vice President and Cabinet Officers are sitting in a working session with Indian leaders is to alleviate some of the cynicism and despair rife among them.

Thus, the Council and the visibility of its Federal members is of great symbolic importance to the Indian people. However, symbolism is not enough. We must be able to report that we have come away from this meeting with commitments on the part of the Federal members that Indian people and their problems will be considered even out of proportion to their numbers or political impact. Otherwise the distrust, the suspicion on the part of the Indians, which has dogged the Federal Government and has defeated most of its attempts to help the Indian people, will continue.

The National Council has a concern with the well-being of

all Indians everywhere—whether they live on the reservations or off; in cities or rural areas; on Federal Indian Reservations or on those established by particular states.

Indian Tribes on Federal reservations have had a very long relationship with the Federal Government. However, in the last decade and a half, longstanding latent suspicion and fear brought about by broken promises, humiliation, and defeat have sharpened into an almost psychological dread of the termination of Federal responsibility. This fear permeates every negotiation, every meeting, every encounter with Indian tribes. Whether this fear can be overcome is debatable, but Federal agencies—especially those represented on this Council—must understand it and be aware of its strangling implications.

Co-existent with this attitude, criticism of the Bureau of Indian Affairs by the Indian people has begun to rise. The criticism has two aspects, the latter of which seems to contradict the opposition to termination.

First, a growing awareness among Indians of how far they have been left behind in achieving the American dream and rising expectations have led to the realization that Bureau services have been grossly inadequate.

Second, a quest for self-determination and control over their own destiny has led to criticism of the paternalistic attitude with which these services have been given in the past. The Indian people are aware that this approach has led to a sense of over-dependency on the Bureau and want to overcome this without losing their special relationship with the Bureau.

In short, the Indian people want more services, more self-determination and relief from the hovering spectre of termination.

The Indian problem has been studied and re-studied, stated and re-stated. There is little need for more study. In 1970, the Indians are entitled to some action, some programs, and some results. To that end we are setting forth a series of specific goals. These goals can and must be met. Such positive federal action will create Indian confidence in the sincerity and capability of the Federal Government.

RECOMMENDATIONS

ADMINISTRATION

Special Assistant to the Secretary

In order to insure parity of opportunity for Indians in all
Federal programs, we recommend that a position in the immediate office of each Departmental Secretary be established
—which hopefully can be filled by an Indian. He will deal
with policy and planning for Indian programs at the central,
regional, and local levels; assure Indian input into legislative
proposals, policy formulation, and program planning; and
report accomplishments on a quarterly basis to the National
Council on Indian Opportunity.

Indian Desks

We recommend that departments establish Indian desks
at the program level.

Assistant Secretary for Indian Affairs

We recommend that the Bureau of Indian Affairs have its
own Assistant Secretary of the Interior, or that the Commissioner of Indian Affairs be given Assistant Secretary status.

Budget

Because no one person knows or is in a position to know
what the various federal departments are planning for Indian
expenditures, we have advised the Executive Director of the
National Council to assign a staff member to acquaint himself with the Indian component in the budget proposals of
the several departments and to follow the budget planning
process through all decision-making levels in the Bureau of
the Budget up to, but not including, the final director's
review.

National Council Field Offices

To insure that the coordinative, evaluative and innovative
responsibilities given to the National Council by the President
are carried out; to maximize delivery of programs at the lowest
local level; and to receive recommendations regarding policy
and programs from local tribes, Indian organizations and individuals, we submit that Council field offices composed of a
Director, Assistant Director, and Administrative Assistant
are essential and must be established in each of the ten Human
Resource Regions.

Demonstration Projects

In order to show that the Government is sincere in its commitments, and to assure greater opportunities available to Indians, we suggest that a demonstration project representing all services available to Indians in each department, be established in order that Indians may observe them and utilize them in their own communities.

BIA In-Service Training

We recommend that the Bureau of Indian Affairs effect as quickly as possible comprehensive in-service training programs to (1) expose all of its employees to the cultural heritages and the value systems of the Indian people they serve and (2) to increase and guarantee the upward mobility of its Indian employees.

Evaluation of BIA Staffing

We recommend that the administrative structure of the BIA be analyzed to determine areas of over-staffing and duplication—with a view toward elimination of "dead wood."

Indian Service on Federal Committees

We recommend that there be equal opportunity for Indians to serve on all appropriate Federal boards, councils, commissions, etc., (e.g., Equal Employment Opportunity, the President's Council on Youth Opportunity, the Civil Rights Commission, etc.).

Indian Youth

The Indian members of the Council recognize the value of having the input of young Indians at policy making levels and in the operation of programs. We recommend that each department give specific attention to the establishment of a federal intern program for young Indians at the local, regional and national levels.

EDUCATION

It is an appalling fact that between 50 and 60% of all Indian children drop out of school. In some areas the figure is as high as 75%. This stands in sharp contrast to the national average of 23%. The suicide rate among all young Indians is over three times the national average. Estimates place it at five to seven times the national average for boarding school students.

A full generation of Indian adults have been severely damaged by an unresponsive and destructive educational system. At a time when economic survival in society requires increasing comprehension of both general knowledge and technical skills, Indians are lost at the lowest level of achievement of any group within our society. We must not lose this generation of Indian children as well. There is a desperate need for both a massive infusion of funds and complete restructuring of basic educational concepts. Therefore, the Indian members of this Council strongly recommend the following major policy initiatives:

1. That a COMPREHENSIVE INDIAN EDUCATION ACT be submitted to Congress to meet the special education needs of Indians in both Federal and public schools in an effective and coordinated manner. This act will pull together all Indian education programs including set-aside programs. Provision would be made for Indian input, contracting authority with tribes and communities, submission of plans, accountability and evaluation procedures in the hope of correcting the glaring inadequacies and misdirections that exist in present programs such as the Johnson-O'Malley Act. . . .

2. That the Civil Rights Enforcement Office of HEW investigate discrimination against Indians in schools receiving federal funds.

3. That a permanent Indian education subcommittee be established in each house of the Congress.

4. That funding for Indian education be substantially increased. Funds at present are not adequate for even basic rudimentary requirements such as reasonable teacher-student and dormitory counselor-student ratios. It is a fact today that the average student-counselor ratio in BIA boarding schools is one to 60 during the day and one to 150 at night. Innovative program planning and implementation cannot be successfully carried out without the support of basic operational facilities and staff.

5. That the present reorganization of the BIA assign to the

assistant commissioner for education the responsibilities of a superintendent of federal schools, having direct line control over the operation of the schools, including budgets, personnel systems and supporting services.

6. That the Bilingual Education Act receive sufficient funding so that an expanded program would be available for Indian and Eskimo children, including those at schools operated for Indians by nonprofit institutions, and that the BIA undertake an expanded bilingual program of its own. This program can and should include the hiring of a greatly increased number of Indian teacher aides.

7. That courses in Indian languages, history and culture be established in all Indian schools including those slated for transfer to state control, and that a revision of textbooks be undertaken to make them relevant to an Indian child's experience and to eliminate derogatory references to his heritage.

8. That phasing out of BIA boarding schools become a policy goal. At present approximately 40,000 Indian children attend BIA boarding schools; 9,000 of these children are nine years of age or under. Additional students are housed in BIA bordertown dormitories while they attend off-reservation public schools. These children are often sent several hundred miles from home (in case of Alaskan children thousands of miles) due to the lack of facilities in their area. The schools which they attend are often emotionally disturbing and culturally destructive to some children and their families and are educationally deficient as well. In order to eliminate boarding schools, roads must be constructed in rural areas; without sufficient road appropriations there cannot be realistic access to schools for these children on a daily attendance basis. A plan must be developed for the construction of a vast network of community schools and the present allocation of money for construction at existing boarding schools must be reallocated to the construction of community based schools.

9. That tribal control of schools with the continuation of federal funding be implemented upon the request of Indian communities. In conjunction with this, a report should be

submitted by the BIA on the progress that has been made in the establishment of local Indian school boards and the powers which have been granted to these boards. The time has come for an end to the solely advisory role that has been played by the majority of these boards. The OEO-BIA joint experiment at the Rough Rock School on the Navajo Reservation has shown that Indian control is both a feasible and desirable means of operation. Community located and controlled schools could also serve as adult education centers and would help to acquaint Indian parents with the importance of their involvement in the education of their children in a setting with which they can identify.

10. That training programs in Indian cultures and value systems be provided to teachers, administrators and dormitory counselors—be they Anglo or Indian. There is no excuse for a quiet, shy Indian child being labeled and treated as dumb and unresponsive by an uncomprehending teacher.

11. That the need for a far greater number of Indian teachers must be recognized. At present, there are far too few Indians graduating from college to meet this need. Increased availability of scholarships to Indian students would enable a greater number to attend institutions of higher education. We support the establishment of a national scholarship clearinghouse for Indian students which would include the contracting of the BIA scholarship program. In order to obtain the highest quality teachers we recommend the elimination of the Civil Service regulation that protects by tenure incompetent and prejudiced teachers from dismissal.

12. That Federal funds be provided for the establishment of tribal community colleges.

13. That, recognizing the first five years of life as being of great importance in proper child development, there be an expansion of HEADSTART and kindergarten programs for Indian schools rather than a reduction. We also stress the necessity for a continuous process of Indian input into their organization and operation.

14. That modern educational communication techniques

be utilized to enhance the educational opportunities for all Indian people.

HEALTH

It is a recognized fact that despite considerable improvement the health status of the American Indian is far below that of the general population of the United States. Indian infant mortality after the first month of life is three times the national average. This means, in plain language, that children are dying needlessly. The average life span of Indians is 44 years, one-third short of the national average of 64 years; in Alaska it is only 36 years. In light of the dire need for all health facilities and health needs, it is criminal to impose a personnel and budget freeze on Indian health programs. Even without a freeze, Indian hospitals are woefully understaffed and under supplied, even to the extent of lacking basic equipment and medicine. We deplore the budget decisions that have caused this state of inadequacy.

There are a number of specific actions that can be taken now to improve Indian health services:

1. An Indian health aide program has been established. A review should be undertaken of its recruitment, training and assignment policies.

2. The Division of Indian Health and the regular U.S. Public Health Service should establish communication for ascertaining their respective areas of responsibility. There is no excuse for the plight of a sick individual, who also happens to be Indian, to be denied access to health facilities due to jurisdictional conflicts.

3. The establishment of Indian advisory boards at hospitals should be continued and expanded. However, to be meaningful, these boards must be given actual authority in the administrative areas of patient care.

4. The establishment of a program to bring Indian health services into communities rather than simply at the central office location, e.g., traveling clinics.

5. Lastly, the Council goes on record in support of a national health insurance system.

WELFARE

President Nixon's proposal for a Family Assistance Program is a major step toward restoring dignity to the individuals involved. We support the concept of this program and urge its enactment and adequate funding. We also request Indian input into its planning and delivery, for without a mutual exchange this new, innovative program will not satisfy the unique needs of the Indian people.

We specifically recommend today the following:

1. That an immediate investigation be undertaken of the system whereby many welfare recipients are exploited by trading post and grocery store owners. These trading posts and grocery stores are the mailing address for large numbers of Indian welfare recipients in the surrounding areas. By isolated location, overcharging and credit, and the custom of dependency, the traders and store owners have complete control over the disbursement of the welfare checks;

2. That training programs in the culture and value systems of the Indian populations be required for social workers serving Indian people;

3. That Indian tribes be given the option of contracting with the Federal government for the administration of their own welfare programs.

URBAN

A National Council on Indian Opportunity study conducted in 1968–69 has found that one-half of the Indian population in the United States is located in urban areas. Yet none of the programs of the Federal government are aimed with any meaningful impact on the special problems which Indians in these urban environments face.

A majority of the urban Indians have arrived at their present location through the Federal government's relocation program. This program is seriously deficient in funds and in professional direction for economic, social and psychological adjustment to an environment that is almost totally strange, impersonal and alien. Aside from budgetary considerations, this raises the fundamental question of whether relocation is a proper policy or goal. In the study group's hearings, those Indians who testified expressed deep hostility for the program, its administrators, and its fallacious inducements' After serious analysis based on the hearings, the Indian Council members have concluded that viable economic development on or near present Indian communities is a goal much preferable to the artificial movement of individuals or families.

Immediate action must be taken to re-evaluate the entire jurisdiction of this relocation policy. In addition, the needed services for these people presently situated in these urban societies must be created and it is therefore recommended that the following actions be taken:

1. The Departments of Commerce, HEW, HUD, and OEO must educate themselves to the location of urban Indian concentrations with the purpose of bringing their present services directly and effectively into these areas. In addition, they must develop new programs and initiatives to answer the special needs of Indians in an urban environment.

2. Reinforcement of existing urban Indian centers and active support for the development of new centers located in neighborhood Indian areas which would serve the two-fold purpose of community centers and programmatic referral agencies.

3. Establishment of legal aid offices in Indian ghetto areas.

ECONOMIC DEVELOPMENT

Indian people in general have been deprived of the opportunity of obtaining business acumen and have not participated in the benefits of the American free enterprise system. This fact has led to the present economic plight of the first Americans and has been an embarrassment to principles upon which this country was founded. But in recent years, because of a cooperative effort involving government agencies and of the private groups, industrial development on Indian reservations is starting to become a reality. This development is greatly desired by most tribes to improve the economics of the communities and to provide jobs for the individuals of those communities.

However, where large industries have located in Indian communities, the inadequacies of the reservation to accommodate the sudden concentration of employee populations have created serious problems. In most of these new industrial communities there are inadequate schools, too few houses, insufficient hospital and medical capability and generally inadequate community facilities for the population. While Indians desire and deserve job opportunities near their homes, most of the industries thus far attracted to reservations have chiefly employed women. This leaves the male head of the family still unemployed and disrupts the family. Attention of those federal agencies concerned with industrial development should be directed to this problem and they should maximize employment for Indian men.

Most of the industries which locate in Indian country are subsidized by the government because they are to provide jobs for Indians. The government should make employment of a high percentage of Indians a condition of the federal subsidy to ensure increased Indian employment.

High on the list of impediments to industrialization on Indian reservations is the lack of hard surfaced roads. Roads will have to be developed to handle the traffic of the work force and to provide a way to market goods produced and to procure necessary supplies.

A curious ruling of the Federal Aviation Agency is that Indian tribes are not public bodies. The legislation authorizing federal assistance in construction of airports limits that assistance to public bodies thereby excluding Indian tribes who wish to construct airports.

Finally, we wish to go on record supporting proposed legislation which would provide tax incentives to industry locating on Indian reservations. An exemption of industry from federal taxation for a period of years would provide much needed inducement to industry to come to Indian reservations. With regard to helping individual Indians into business for themselves, programs providing the necessary capital through loans at low interest rates and continuing technical assistance are essential to success.

Work must be done to create a climate and receptivity among Indian individuals to go into business and there must be a sustained vehicle to accomplish this if Indians are to overcome their lack of experience in business management. To complement this effort there is a need for developing a greater number of business opportunities. A program of sustained management and technical assistance as well as adequate financing is needed. A talent search is needed to locate and identify the potential Indian entrepreneur.

Therefore we recommend:

1. That there be developed a program of a 100% secured loan program for five years for Indians.

2. That there be attempts with the American Bankers Association with federal program linkage to develop training to familiarize bankers with special and unique needs of the Indian communities and to involve selected Indians in banking training programs.

3. That a consumer education program be developed and implemented for all Indians.

4. That an Indian program to establish Indian credit unions and to implement credit union management training for Indians be organized and funded.

LEGAL

Independent Indian Legal Agency

Government lawyers in the Interior and Justice Departments handling Indian legal rights are caught in a conflict because they also represent government agencies in litigation affecting Indian rights. In many cases government lawyers have failed to pursue untested legal claims of the tribes that would yield substantial water rights.

Because of this conflict, we recommend the establishment of an agency independent from both the Interior and Justice Departments to represent the tribes in all legal services required in connection with all Indian rights to lands, water, and natural resources.

Jurisdiction

At the present time Indian tribal courts do not have jurisdiction over non-Indian offenders on their reservations. In order to adequately control and develop these reservations, such jurisdiction must be extended to them where such an extension is desired by the tribes. Further research and study of this problem is needed. A further report suggesting how this study might be conducted will be forthcoming from the National Council on Indian Opportunity to the Interior and Justice Departments.

Alaska Native Land Rights

The enactment by Congress, in its current session, of legislation for the equitable settlement of the land rights of the Natives of Alaska—the Eskimos, Indians, and Aleuts—is of highest priority. Justice requires that the settlement embrace the proposals set forth by the Alaska Federation of Natives which contemplates:

1. That fee simple title be confirmed in the Alaska Natives to a fair part of their ancestral lands.

2. That just compensation for the lands taken from the Natives include not only cash but also a continuing royalty share in the revenues derived from the resources of such lands.

We urge that the several departments of the government, and in particular the Secretaries of Interior and Agriculture, and the Bureau of the Budget, reassess their position and give their full support to the proposal of the Alaska Federation of Natives.

AGRICULTURE

Indian members of the National Council on Indian Opportunity strongly urge the Farmers Home Administration to re-emphasize its efforts to make economic opportunity and low-income housing loans available to Indians in rural areas. This effort can be aided a great deal by employing Indians as field workers in areas with high Indian concentration. FHA should work closely with the Bureau of Indian Affairs to find a way to adjust its security requirements to the unique Indian situation. This will ensure that more loans will be made to Indians residing on trust land.

We commend the Extension Service for providing 60 professional extension workers in 17 states and 90 Indian aides on reservations and in Indian communities to explain and demonstrate nutrition programs and better use of resources to attain a better quality of living. (Expanded assistance to urban Indians should be emphasized in the future.) Plans should proceed for conducting seminars and short courses for Indians on household management, budgeting and credit, and improved methods of breeding, feeding, and marketing of livestock.

The Farmer Cooperative Service assistance to Alaskan Native cooperatives and Indian cooperatives in Oklahoma has been very useful. We request that this service actively seek out opportunities for the use of cooperatives among Indian farmers and provide the technical assistance to keep the cooperatives afloat.

The Soil Conservation Service can provide an important service for Indians because land is their most valuable remaining resource. Wherever the Soil Conservation Service can cooperate with the Interior Department in preserving Indian land from erosion and flood it should actively offer to do so. Interior Department resources for soil and water conservation do not appear to be adequate to meet the total Indian need.

The Agricultural Stabilization and Conservation Service also provides an important service in encouraging soil and water conservation practices. This technical assistance should be made available to all Indian farmers. The federal payments for wool produced and marketed by Indians, especially in Arizona and New Mexico, is a beneficial program and efforts should be made to assure that all Indians eligible for these payments are made aware of the program.

The Donation Feed Program in Agriculture had no authority to purchase hay for starving Papago cattle in 1968, and as a result the tribal herd was devastated. If the weakened cattle had been able to consume Departmentally owned feed grain they would have been saved. The Department should not allow such a disaster to be repeated.

The Department of Agriculture has several other programs which can assist Indian progress. Without going into detail, the Consumer and Marketing Service, the Economic Research Service, Agricultural Research Service, Rural Electrification Administration, Food and Nutrition Service, and the Forest Service are useful to Indians, but special efforts should be made to improve the availability of services to Indians.

HOUSING

Housing among American Indians and Eskimos is deplorable. It is worse than that found in Appalachia or any slum. That this situation should exist in America in 1970, when many Americans are becoming two-home owner families, is a cruel paradox. Immediate action must be given by Federal departments to relieve this blight.

Even though some small breakthrough has been made in Indian housing, the need remaining is tremendous. There needs to be a review of financing to provide increased Indian participation in all housing programs. During the past year, a tri-agency agreement involving the Departments of Interior, HEW, and HUD was effected to provide for coordination of expanded housing and expanded Indian water and sanitation facilities programs. This represents an effort to seek a better way of dealing with difficult problems by a joint effort. However, these efforts need to be reviewed to increase production and emphasis and to maintain action.

We recommend, in order to put the Indian housing problem into clearer focus, that regional conferences be held with a cross-section of Indian representatives and appropriate Federal regional administrators, to determine what can practically and effectively be done with support of tribes and Indian organizations. These conferences should touch on the following needs:
- greater flexibility in determining types of housing programs appropriate to a situation.
- a review of the effectiveness and status of housing authorities.

• in cooperation with lending agencies, an analysis of the default rate and the causes for it.

We also point out that a solution to the Indian housing problem will help to solve corollary problems—family instability, health and sanitation problems, poor school attendance or even dropouts, juvenile delinquency, and others.

BLUE LAKE

For more than 60 years the Taos Pueblo Indians have been seeking—by peaceful and legal means—the return of their religious sanctuary—Blue Lake. Because the problem is unique and because it has persisted over so many decades, we feel that the Taos struggle merits the special attention of the Council.

In 1965 the Indian Claims Commission ruled that the Blue Lake area and an additional 130,000 acres were seized illegally. However, the Taos Indians are seeking the return of only the area containing the ancient shrine and holy places of their religion.

Once again, a bill introduced in Congress which would right this injustice has passed the House of Representatives and is pending in the Senate. We recommend that the full Council support this legislation and hope that Council members, individually will support the Taos Pueblo at every opportunity.

January 26, 1970

Mr. Vice President, Members of the Cabinet, Members of the National Council on Indian Opportunity, and Guests:

We have had presented this afternoon a rather lengthy recitation of the ills that beset the American Indian. You will appreciate that the needs of the Indian people are quite extensive but you must also appreciate that they do not have universal application to all Indian tribes everywhere.

On behalf of the Navajo Indian, I feel that there must be

a more specific treatment of his problem, and in making this presentation, I realize that it may have specific application to other Indian tribes as well as the Navajo Tribe.

The foremost need of all Indian people is a steady, income-producing job. For without this, the Indian is forced to live on a day-to-day basis with no economic security whatever. You are all aware, however, that mass employment is possible chiefly through the acquisition of industry. You are also aware that industry is fiercely sought by every city, town, and hamlet through the United States.

For the past six years, the Navajo has turned his attention assiduously to securing industry, and, to a measure, has been successful. But, these industries are all too few to take up the slack of the unemployed Navajo who number some 35,000 of a total population of some 140,000.

The Navajo, however, has been able to dispel the time-worn idea that the American Indian is a drunk and incapable of providing continuous and steady employment. By reason of the work of the Navajo, there are now some 22 industries actually seeking to locate on the Navajo Reservation. We would, of course, like to be able to furnish the facilities for all of these industries, but our limited economic resources preclude this.

As you know, industries, in the main, will locate in a particular area only if the facilities are built by the community seeking them and leased on favorable terms.

How then, can Indian people secure industries in this competitive labor market? Specifically, I would suggest that the Cabinet seriously consider asking Congress to set aside an industrial fund for the use of Indian Tribes. I would further suggest that an initial sum of $100 million be appropriated for this purpose. But, let me hasten to explain that this is not a "handout." Rather, the money would be loaned to the particular Tribe at a favorable rate of interest. The Tribe would then lease the facility and pay over the lease rental directly to the Federal agency involved. In this way, the industrial fund would remain intact and would be available for additional use as the need might arise.

I am certain that this would alleviate a great deal of unemployment among the American Indian and it would be a good business proposition for the Federal Government.

I realize that this would not cure the several ills, as so ably set forward in the paper we have received from the National Council on Indian Opportunity, but it would be a giant step in that direction. Given steady employment security, we would then focus on other problems facing the American Indian and perhaps solve these as well. For, with industrial well-being, I am certain that we would be able to find the means for better roads, houses, schools, hospitals, and other needed services.

I want to thank you for the opportunity of appearing before you today and presenting this statement.

Raymond Nakai
Chairman, Navajo Tribe

MESSAGE TO CONGRESS ON INDIAN AFFAIRS

President Richard M. Nixon
July 8, 1970

The long-awaited enunciation of President Nixon's Indian policy came in a special Presidential Message to Congress on Indian Affairs on July 8, 1970.

In many respects it was a logical culmination of all that had occurred and all that had been recommended in Indian affairs during the preceding decade. But in the full context of Indian-white relations in the United States, it was historic in tone and intent. It was a firm rebuttal by a Chief Executive of the nation of the white man's conviction — countenanced officially for many generations — that the Indians were incompetent to control their own affairs. It proclaimed for the executive branch of the government the Indians' right to self-determination and urged the Congress to join in making it the nation's policy and the official yardstick by which to measure future federal-Indian relations. It was the strongest assertion yet made by any President against the twin evils of paternalism and termination. And in its many proposals for dealing with reservation life, tribal grievances, and Indian demands to continue as Indians and manage their own affairs themselves, it showed that a national administration had at last listened to the Indians and accepted *their* ideas of what they needed and wanted. It would no longer be "either-or" for the Indians (be either a white man or an Indian). Forced assimilation into the mainstream, the most benign aim of the white man for Indians since colonial days, would be abandoned by President Nixon.

The message, however, was no more than a statement of intent. It did not, by itself, bring about self-determination or any of the measures it proposed. It created no new conditions on the reservations, and it did not halt abruptly the paternalism of the Bureau of Indian Affairs. But it pointed federal policy in a new direction and demanded new thinking and attitudes from those in the federal agencies who dealt in Indian affairs.

The Indians' response to the President's message was guarded. Most of them were pleased with its theme of self-determination, but they were skeptical whether the administration would take action to implement the words. Actions did follow. Administration bills, prepared with the participation of the Indian members of the National Council on Indian Opportunity, were introduced into Congress to carry out the major provisions of the message. Again the Indians were wary. The tribes had had no hand in framing the measures, and history had taught them to be guarded about what Washington officials decided was best for them. Even the Indians who found they could support the bills adopted a "watch and wait" attitude to see with what degree of commitment the administration would bring its persuasive powers to bear on Congress in behalf of the measures.

Meanwhile, the National Council on Indian Opportunity conducted two series of meetings with Indians around the country to discuss the bills and allow the Indians to recommend revisions in them or suggest new measures. And late in November the Bureau of Indian Affairs announced dramatic changes, formulated with the help of its Indian task forces, in structure, procedures, and philosophy designed to accelerate the attainment of Indian self-determination. The changes coincided almost exactly with demands that Indians had been making since 1961. They included the redelegation of decision-making authorities from the area offices to the reservation level; the change of name and job description of the reservation "superintendent" to "field administrator," reflecting the shift of the bureau as a whole from the management of Indian affairs to the servicing of Indian needs; the reassignment of bureau personnel and the institution of rotation policies that would encourage better federal-Indian relations; the formalizing of procedures by which tribes could take control, with federal funding, of their own affairs; and the establishment of evaluation and inspection programs. In sum, the bureau changes, coupled with the legislation stemming from the President's message, set the stage at last for the realization of self-determination, and there could be no turning back. By making contracts to administer themselves all the programs formerly run for them by the Bureau of Indian Affairs, the Zuñi of New Mexico earlier in 1970 had already become the first tribe to take control of their own affairs. Now the so-called Zuñi plan could be adopted for all or part of their programs by other tribes, and by early December, 1970, the bureau had almost thirty requests by Indian groups in different parts of the country to take over control of some or all of their own affairs.

It was, of course, only a start. The President's message and the bureau changes were large and historic steps forward. But the Indians were still "the poorest of the poor." Social, economic, health, housing, and educational problems still beset every reservation. Aggressive white interests, including planners of government projects, still threatened Indian land, water, and other resources. Dictatorial bureaucrats and paternalistic white "experts" still held the upper hand on many reservations. Injustices and discrimination had not suddenly disappeared. In short, Indian Americans still faced a long struggle to attain the freedoms and standards of living enjoyed by all other Americans. Following is the text of President Nixon's Indian Affairs Message.

TO THE CONGRESS OF THE UNITED STATES:

The first Americans—the Indians—are the most deprived and most isolated minority group in our nation. On virtually every scale of measurement—employment, income, education, health—the condition of the Indian people ranks at the bottom.

This condition is the heritage of centuries of injustice. From the time of their first contact with European settlers, the American Indians have been oppressed and brutalized, deprived of their ancestral lands and denied the opportunity to control their own destiny. Even the Federal programs which are intended to meet their needs have frequently proven to be ineffective and demeaning.

But the story of the Indian in America is something more than the record of the white man's frequent aggression, broken agreements, intermittent remorse and prolonged failure. It is a record also of endurance, of survival, of adaptation and creativity in the face of overwhelming obstacles. It is a record of enormous contributions to this country—to its art and culture, to its strength and spirit, to its sense of history and its sense of purpose.

It is long past time that the Indian policies of the Federal government began to recognize and build upon the capacities and insights of the Indian people. Both as a matter of justice and as a matter of enlightened social policy, we must begin to act on the basis of what the Indians themselves have long been telling us. The time has come to break decisively with the past and to create the conditions for a new era in which the Indian future is determined by Indian acts and Indian decisions.

Self-Determination Without Termination

The first and most basic question that must be answered with respect to Indian policy concerns the historic and legal relationship between the Federal government and Indian communities. In the past, this relationship has oscillated between two equally harsh and unacceptable extremes.

On the one hand, it has—at various times during previous Administrations—been the stated policy objective of both the Executive and Legislative branches of the Federal government eventually to terminate the trusteeship relationship between the Federal government and the Indian people. As recently as August of 1953, in House Concurrent Resolution 108, the Congress declared that termination was the long-range goal of its Indian policies. This would mean that Indian tribes would eventually lose any special standing they had under Federal law; the tax exempt status of their lands would be discontinued; Federal responsibility for their economic and social well-being would be repudiated; and the tribes themselves would be effectively dismantled. Tribal property would be divided among individual members who would then be assimilated into the society at large.

This policy of forced termination is wrong, in my judgment, for a number of reasons. First, the premises on which it rests are wrong. Termination implies that the Federal government has taken on a trusteeship responsibility for Indian communities as an act of generosity toward a disadvantaged people and that it can therefore discontinue this responsibility on a unilateral basis whenever it sees fit. But the unique status of Indian tribes does not rest on any premise such as this. The special relationship between Indians and the Federal government is the result instead of solemn obligations which have been entered into by the United States Government. Down through the years, through written treaties and through formal and informal agreements, our government has made specific commitments to the Indian people. For their part, the Indians have often surrendered claims to vast tracts of land and have accepted life on government reservations. In exchange, the government has agreed to provide community services such as health, education and public safety, services which would presumably allow Indian communities to enjoy a standard of living comparable to that of other Americans.

This goal, of course, has never been achieved. But the special relationship between the Indian tribes and the Federal government which arises from these agreements continues to carry immense moral and legal force. To terminate this relationship would be no more appropriate than to terminate the citizenship rights of any other American.

The second reason for rejecting forced termination is that the practical results have been clearly harmful in the few instances in which termination actually has been tried. The removal of Federal trusteeship responsibility has produced considerable disorientation among the affected Indians and has left them unable to relate to a myriad of Federal, State and local assistance efforts. Their economic and social condition has often been worse after termination than it was before.

The third argument I would make against forced termination concerns the effect it has had upon the overwhelming majority of tribes which still enjoy a special relationship with the Federal government. The very threat that this relationship may someday be ended has created a great deal of apprehension among Indian groups and this apprehension, in turn, has had a blighting effect on tribal progress. Any step that might result in greater social, economic or political autonomy is regarded with suspicion by many Indians who fear that it will only bring them closer to the day when the Federal government will disavow its responsibility and cut them adrift.

In short, the fear of one extreme policy, forced termination, has often worked to produce the opposite extreme: excessive dependence on the Federal government. In many cases this dependence is so great that the Indian community is almost entirely run by outsiders who are responsible and responsive to Federal officials in Washington, D.C., rather than to the communities they are supposed to be serving. This is the second of the two harsh approaches which have long plagued our Indian policies. Of the Department of the Interior's programs directly serving Indians, for example, only 1.5 percent are presently under Indian control. Only 2.4 percent of HEW's Indian health programs are run by Indians. The result is a burgeoning Federal bureaucracy, programs which are far less effective than they ought to be, and an erosion of Indian initiative and morale.

I believe that both of these policy extremes are wrong. Federal termination errs in one direction, Federal paternalism errs in the other. Only by clearly rejecting both of these extremes can we achieve a policy which truly serves the best interests of the Indian people. Self-determination among the Indian people can and must be encouraged without the threat of eventual termination. In my view, in fact, that is the only way that self-determination can effectively be fostered.

This, then, must be the goal of any new national policy toward the Indian people: to strengthen the Indian's sense of autonomy without threatening his sense of community. We must assure the Indian that he can assume control of his own life without being separated involuntarily from the tribal group. And we must make it clear that Indians can become independent of Federal control without being cut off from Federal concern and Federal support. My specific recommendations to the Congress are designed to carry out this policy.

1. *Rejecting Termination*

Because termination is morally and legally unacceptable, because it produces bad practical results, and because the mere threat of termination tends to discourage greater self-sufficiency among Indian groups, I am asking the Congress to pass a new Concurrent Resolution which would expressly renounce, repudiate and repeal the termination policy as expressed in House Concurrent Resolution 108 of the 83rd Congress. This resolution would explicitly affirm the integrity and right to continued existence of all Indian tribes and Alaska native governments, recognizing that cultural pluralism is a source of national strength. It would assure these groups that the United States Government would continue to carry out its treaty and trusteeship obligations to them as long as the groups themselves believed that such a policy was necessary or desirable. It would guarantee that whenever Indian groups decided to assume control or responsibility for government service programs, they could do so and still receive adequate Federal financial support. In short, such a resolution would reaffirm for the Legislative branch—as I hereby affirm for the

Executive branch—that the historic relationship between the Federal government and the Indian communities cannot be abridged without the consent of the Indians.

2. *The Right to Control and Operate Federal Programs*

Even as we reject the goal of forced termination, so must we reject the suffocating pattern of paternalism. But how can we best do this? In the past, we have often assumed that because the government is obliged to provide certain services for Indians, it therefore must administer those same services. And to get rid of Federal administration, by the same token, often meant getting rid of the whole Federal program. But there is no necessary reason for this assumption. Federal support programs for non-Indian communities—hospitals and schools are two ready examples—are ordinarily administered by local authorities. There is no reason why Indian communities should be deprived of the privilege of self-determination merely because they receive monetary support from the Federal government. Nor should they lose Federal money because they reject Federal control.

For years we have talked about encouraging Indians to exercise greater self-determination, but our progress has never been commensurate with our promises. Part of the reason for this situation has been the threat of termination. But another reason is the fact that when a decision is made as to whether a Federal program will be turned over to Indian administration, it is the Federal authorities and not the Indian people who finally make that decision.

This situation should be reversed. In my judgment, it should be up to the Indian tribe to determine whether it is willing and able to assume administrative responsibility for a service program which is presently administered by a Federal agency. To this end, I am proposing legislation which would empower a tribe or a group of tribes or any other Indian community to take over the control or operation of Federally-funded and administered programs in the Department of the Interior and the Department of Health, Education and Welfare whenever the tribal council or comparable community governing group voted to do so.

Under this legislation, it would not be necessary for the Federal agency administering the program to approve the transfer of responsibility. It is my hope and expectation that most such transfers of power would still take place consensually as a result of negotiations between the local community and the Federal government. But in those cases in which an impasse arises between the two parties, the final determination should rest with the Indian community.

Under the proposed legislation, Indian control of Indian programs would always be a wholly voluntary matter. It would be possible for an Indian group to select that program or that specified portion of a program that it wants to run without assuming responsibility for other components. The "right of retrocession" would also be guaranteed; this means that if the local community elected to administer a program and then later decided to give it back to the Federal government, it would always be able to do so.

Appropriate technical assistance to help local organizations successfully operate these programs would be provided by the Federal government. No tribe would risk economic disadvantage from managing its own programs; under the proposed legislation, locally-administered programs would be funded on equal terms with similar services still administered by Federal authorities. The legislation I propose would include appropriate protections against any action which endangered the rights, the health, the safety or the welfare of individuals. It would also contain accountability procedures to guard against gross negligence or mismanagement of Federal funds.

This legislation would apply only to services which go directly from the Federal government to the Indian community; those services which are channeled through State or local governments could still be turned over to Indian control by mutual consent. To run the activities for which they have assumed control, the Indian groups could employ local people or outside experts. If they chose to hire Federal employees who had formerly administered these projects, those employees would still enjoy the privileges of Federal employee benefit programs—under special legislation which will also be submitted to the Congress.

Legislation which guarantees the right of Indians to contract for the control or operation of Federal programs would directly channel more money into Indian communities, since Indians themselves would be administering programs and drawing salaries which now often go to non-Indian administrators. The potential for Indian control is significant, for we are talking about programs which annually spend over $400 million in Federal funds. A policy which encourages Indian administration of these programs will help build greater pride and resourcefulness within the Indian community. At the same time, programs which are managed and operated by Indians are likely to be more effective in meeting Indian needs.

I speak with added confidence about these anticipated results because of the favorable experience of programs which have already been turned over to Indian control. Under the auspices of the Office of Economic Opportunity, Indian communities now run more than 60 community action agencies which are located on Federal reservations. OEO is planning to spend some $57 million in Fiscal Year 1971 through Indian-controlled grantees. For over four years, many OEO-funded programs have operated under the control of local Indian organizations and the results have been most heartening.

Two Indian tribes—the Salt River Tribe and the Zuñi Tribe—have recently extended this principle of local control to virtually all of the programs which the Bureau of Indian Affairs has traditionally administered for them. Many Federal officials, including the Agency Superintendent, have been replaced by elected tribal officers or tribal employees. The time has now come to build on these experiences and to extend local Indian control—at a rate and to the degree that the Indians themselves establish.

3. *Restoring the Sacred Lands Near Blue Lake*

No government policy toward Indians can be fully effective unless there is a relationship of trust and confidence between the Federal government and the Indian people. Such a relationship cannot be completed overnight; it is inevitably the product of a long series of words and actions. But we can contribute significantly to such a relationship by responding to just grievances which are especially important to the Indian people.

One such grievance concerns the sacred Indian lands at and near Blue Lake in New Mexico. From the fourteenth century, the Taos Pueblo Indians used these areas for religious and tribal purposes. In 1906, however, the United States Government appropriated these lands for the creation of a national forest. According to a recent determination of the Indian Claims Commission, the government "took said lands from petitioner without compensation."

For 64 years, the Taos Pueblo has been trying to regain possession of this sacred lake and watershed area in order to preserve it in its natural condition and limit its non-Indian use. The Taos Indians consider such action essential to the protection and expression of their religious faith.

The restoration of the Blue Lake lands to the Taos Pueblo Indians is an issue of unique and critical importance to Indians throughout the country. I therefore take this opportunity wholeheartedly to endorse legislation which would restore 48,000 acres of sacred land to the Taos Pueblo people, with the statutory promise that they would be able to use these lands for traditional purposes and that except for such uses the lands would remain forever wild.

With the addition of some perfecting amendments, legislation now pending in the Congress would properly achieve this goal. That legislation (H.R. 471) should promptly be amended and enacted. Such action would stand as an important symbol of this government's responsiveness to the just grievances of the American Indians.

4. *Indian Education*

One of the saddest aspects of Indian life in the United States is the low quality of Indian education. Drop-out rates for Indians are twice the national average and the average educational level for all Indians under Federal supervision is less than six school years. Again, at least a part of the problem stems from the fact that the Federal government is trying to do for Indians what many Indians could do better for themselves.

The Federal government now has responsibility for some 221,000 Indian children of school age. While over 50,000 of these children attend schools which are operated directly by the Bureau of Indian Affairs, only 750 Indian children are enrolled in schools where the responsibility for education has been contracted by the BIA to Indian school boards. Fortunately, this condition is beginning to change. The Ramah Navajo Community of New Mexico and the Rough Rock and Black Water Schools in Arizona are notable examples of schools which have recently been brought under local Indian control. Several other communities are now negotiating for similar arrangements.

Consistent with our policy that the Indian community should have the right to take over the control and operation of federally funded programs, we believe every Indian community wishing to do so should be able to control its own Indian schools. This control would be exercised by school boards selected by Indians and functioning much like other school boards throughout the nation. To assure that this goal is achieved, I am asking the Vice President, acting in his role as Chairman of the National Council on Indian Opportunity, to establish a Special Education Subcommittee of that Council. The members of that Subcommittee should be Indian educators who are selected by the Council's Indian members. The Subcommittee will provide technical assistance to Indian communities wishing to establish school boards, will conduct a nationwide review of the educational status of all Indian school children in whatever schools they may be attending, and will evaluate and report annually on the status of Indian education, including the extent of local control. This Subcommittee will act as a transitional mechanism; its objective should not be self-perpetuation but the actual transfer of Indian education to Indian communities.

We must also take specific action to benefit Indian children in public schools. Some 141,000 Indian children presently attend general public schools near their homes. Fifty-two thousand of these are absorbed by local school districts without special Federal aid. But 89,000 Indian children attend public schools in such high concentrations that the State or local school districts involved are eligible for special Federal assistance under the Johnson-O'Malley Act. In Fiscal Year 1971, the Johnson-O'Malley program will be funded at a level of some $20 million.

This Johnson-O'Malley money is designed to help Indian students, but since funds go directly to the school districts, the Indians have little if any influence over the way in which the money is spent. I therefore propose that the Congress amend the Johnson-O'Malley Act so as to authorize the Secretary of the Interior to channel funds under this act directly to Indian tribes and communities. Such a provision would give Indians the ability to help shape the schools which their children attend and, in some instances, to set up new school systems of their own. At the same time, I am directing the Secretary of the Interior to make every effort to ensure that Johnson-O'Malley funds which are presently directed to public school districts are actually spent to improve the education of Indian children in these districts.

5. *Economic Development Legislation*

Economic deprivation is among the most serious of Indian problems. Unemployment among Indians is ten times the national average; the unemployment rate runs as high as 80 percent on some of the poorest reservations. Eighty percent of reservation Indians have an income which falls below the poverty line; the average annual income for such families is only $1,500. As I said in September of 1968, it is critically important that the Federal government support and encourage efforts which help Indians develop their own economic infrastructure. To that end, I am proposing the "Indian Financing Act of 1970."

This act would do two things:

1. It would broaden the existing Revolving Loan Fund, which loans money for Indian economic development projects. I am asking that the authorization for this fund be increased from approximately $25 million to $75 million.

2. It would provide additional incentives in the form of

loan guarantees, loan insurance and interest subsidies to encourage *private* lenders to loan more money for Indian economic projects. An aggregate amount of $200 million would be authorized for loan guarantee and loan insurance purposes.

I also urge that legislation be enacted which would permit any tribe which chooses to do so to enter into leases of its land for up to 99 years. Indian people now own over 50 million acres of land that is held in trust by the Federal government. In order to compete in attracting investment capital for commercial, industrial and recreational development of these lands, it is essential that the tribes be able to offer long-term leases. Long-term leasing is preferable to selling such property since it enables tribes to preserve the trust ownership of their reservation homelands. But existing law limits the length of time for which many tribes can enter into such leases. Moreover, when long-term leasing is allowed, it has been granted by Congress on a case-by-case basis, a policy which again reflects a deep-rooted pattern of paternalism. The twenty reservations which have already been given authority for long-term leasing have realized important benefits from that privilege and this opportunity should now be extended to all Indian tribes.

Economic planning is another area where our efforts can be significantly improved. The comprehensive economic development plans that have been created by both the Pima-Maricopa and the Zuñi Tribes provide outstanding examples of interagency cooperation in fostering Indian economic growth. The Zuñi Plan, for example, extends for at least five years and involves a total of $55 million from the Departments of Interior, Housing and Urban Development, and Health, Education and Welfare and from the Office of Economic Opportunity and the Economic Development Administration. I am directing the Secretary of the Interior to play an active role in coordinating additional projects of this kind.

6. *More Money for Indian Health*

Despite significant improvements in the past decade and a half, the health of Indian people still lags 20 to 25 years behind that of the general population. The average age at death among Indians is 44 years, about one-third less than the national average. Infant mortality is nearly 50% higher for Indians and Alaska natives than for the population at large; the tuberculosis rate is eight times as high and the suicide rate is twice that of the general population. Many infectious diseases such as trachoma and dysentery that have all but disappeared among other Americans continue to afflict the Indian people.

This Administration is determined that the health status of the first Americans will be improved. In order to initiate expanded efforts in this area, I will request the allocation of an additional $10 million for Indian health programs for the current fiscal year. This strengthened Federal effort will enable us to address ourselves more effectively to those health problems which are particularly important to the Indian community. We understand, for example, that areas of greatest concern to Indians include the prevention and control of alcoholism, the promotion of mental health and the control of middle-ear disease. We hope that the ravages of middle-ear disease—a particularly acute disease among Indians—can be brought under control within five years.

These and other Indian health programs will be most effective if more Indians are involved in running them. Yet— almost unbelievably—we are presently able to identify in this country only 30 physicians and fewer than 400 nurses of Indian descent. To meet this situation, we will expand our efforts to train Indians for health careers.

7. *Helping Urban Indians*

Our new census will probably show that a larger proportion of America's Indians are living off the reservation than ever before in our history. Some authorities even estimate that more Indians are living in cities and towns than are remaining on the reservation. Of those American Indians who are now dwelling in urban areas, approximately three-fourths are living in poverty.

The Bureau of Indian Affairs is organized to serve the 462,000 reservation Indians. The BIA's responsibility does not extend to Indians who have left the reservation, but this point is not always clearly understood. As a result of this misconception, Indians living in urban areas have often lost out on the opportunity to participate in other programs designed for disadvantaged groups. As a first step toward help ing the urban Indians, I am instructing appropriate officials to do all they can to ensure that this misunderstanding is corrected.

But misunderstandings are not the most important problem confronting urban Indians. The biggest barrier faced by those Federal, State and local programs which are trying to serve urban Indians is the difficulty of locating and identifying them. Lost in the anonymity of the city, often cut off from family and friends, many urban Indians are slow to establish new community ties. Many drift from neighborhood to neighborhood; many shuttle back and forth between reservations and urban areas. Language and cultural differences compound these problems. As a result, Federal, State and local programs which are designed to help such persons often miss this most deprived and least understood segment of the urban poverty population.

This Administration is already taking steps which will help remedy this situation. In a joint effort, the Office of Economic Opportunity and the Department of Health, Education and Welfare will expand support to a total of seven urban Indian centers in major cities which will act as links between existing Federal, State and local service programs and the urban Indians. The Departments of Labor, Housing and Urban Development and Commerce have pledged to cooperate with such experimental urban centers and the Bureau of Indian Affairs has expressed its willingness to contract with these centers for the performance of relocation services which assist reservation Indians in their transition to urban employment.

These efforts represent an important beginning in recognizing and alleviating the severe problems faced by urban Indians. We hope to learn a great deal from these projects and to expand our efforts as rapidly as possible. I am directing the Office of Economic Opportunity to lead these efforts.

8. *Indian Trust Counsel Authority*

The United States Government acts as a legal trustee for the land and water rights of American Indians. These rights are often of critical economic importance to the Indian people; frequently they are also the subject of extensive legal dispute. In many of these legal confrontations, the Federal government is faced with an inherent conflict of interest. The Secretary of the Interior and the Attorney General must at the same time advance *both* the *national* interest in the use of land and water rights *and* the *private* interests of Indians in land which the government holds as trustee.

Every trustee has a legal obligation to advance the interests of the beneficiaries of the trust without reservation and with the highest degree of diligence and skill. Under present conditions, it is often difficult for the Department of the Interior and the Department of Justice to fulfill this obligation. No self-respecting law firm would ever allow itself to represent two opposing clients in one dispute; yet the Federal government has frequently found itself in precisely that position. There is considerable evidence that the Indians are the losers when such situations arise. More than that, the credibility of the Federal government is damaged whenever it appears that such a conflict of interest exists.

In order to correct this situation, I am calling on the Congress to establish an Indian Trust Counsel Authority to assure independent legal representation for the Indians' natural resource rights. This Authority would be governed by a three-man board of directors, appointed by the President with the advice and consent of the Senate. At least two of the board members would be Indian. The chief legal officer of the Authority would be designated as the Indian Trust Counsel.

The Indian Trust Counsel Authority would be independent of the Departments of the Interior and Justice and would be expressly empowered to bring suit in the name of the United States in its trustee capacity. The United States would waive its sovereign immunity from suit in connection with litigation involving the Authority.

9. *Assistant Secretary for Indian and Territorial Affairs*

To help guide the implementation of a new national policy concerning American Indians, I am recommending to the Congress the establishment of a new position in the Department of the Interior—Assistant Secretary for Indian and Territorial Affairs. At present, the Commissioner of Indian Affairs reports to the Secretary of the Interior through the Assistant Secretary for Public Land Management—an officer who has many responsibilities in the natural resources area which compete with his concern for Indians. A new Assistant Secretary for Indian and Territorial Affairs would have only one concern—the Indian and territorial people, their land, and their progress and well-being. Secretary Hickel and I both believe this new position represents an elevation of Indian affairs to their proper role within the Department of the Interior and we urge Congress to act favorably on this proposal.

Continuing Programs

Many of the new programs which are outlined in this message have grown out of this Administration's experience with other Indian projects that have been initiated or expanded during the last 17 months.

The Office of Economic Opportunity has been particularly active in the development of new and experimental efforts. OEO's Fiscal Year 1971 budget request for Indian-related activities is up 18 percent from 1969 spending. In the last year alone—to mention just two examples—OEO doubled its funds for Indian economic development and tripled its expenditures for alcoholism and recovery programs. In areas such as housing and home improvement, health care, emergency food, legal services and education, OEO programs have been significantly expanded. As I said in my recent speech on the economy, I hope that the Congress will support this valuable work by appropriating the full amount requested for the Economic Opportunity Act.

The Bureau of Indian Affairs has already begun to implement our policy of contracting with local Indians for the operation of government programs. As I have noted, the Salt River Tribe and the Zuñi Tribe have taken over the bulk of Federal services; other projects ranging from job training centers to high school counseling programs have been contracted out to Indian groups on an individual basis in many areas of the country.

Economic development has also been stepped up. Of 195 commercial and industrial enterprises which have been established in Indian areas with BIA assistance, 71 have come into operation within the last two years. These enterprises provide jobs for more than 6,000 Indians and are expected to employ substantially more when full capacity is reached. A number of these businesses are now owned by Indians and many others are managed by them. To further increase individual Indian ownership, the BIA has this month initiated the Indian Business Development Fund which provides equity capital to Indians who go into business in reservation areas.

Since late 1967, the Economic Development Administration has approved approximately $80 million in projects on Indian reservations, including nearly $60 million in public works projects. The impact of such activities can be tremendous; on the Gila River Reservation in Arizona, for example, economic development projects over the last three years have helped to lower the unemployment rate from 56 to 18 percent, increase the median family income by 150 percent and cut the welfare rate by 50 percent.

There has been additional progress on many other fronts since January of 1969. New "Indian Desks" have been created in each of the human resource departments of the Federal government to help coordinate and accelerate Indian programs. We have supported an increase in funding of $4 million for the Navajo Irrigation Project. Housing efforts have picked up substantially; a new Indian Police Academy has been set up; Indian education efforts have been expanded — including an increase of $848,000 in scholarships for Indian college students and the establishment of the Navajo Community College, the first college in America planned, developed and operated by and for Indians. Altogether, obligational authority for Indian programs run by the Federal Government has increased from a little over $598 million in Fiscal Year 1970 to almost $626 million in Fiscal Year 1971.

Finally, I would mention the impact on the Indian population of the series of welfare reform proposals I have sent to the Congress. Because of the high rate of unemployment and underemployment among Indians, there is probably no other group in the country that would be helped as directly and as substantially by programs such as the new Family Assistance Plan and the proposed Family Health Insurance Plan. It is estimated, for example, that more than half of all Indian families would be eligible for Family Assistance benefits and the enactment of this legislation is therefore of critical importance to the American Indian.

This Administration has broken a good deal of new ground with respect to Indian problems in the last 17 months. We have learned many things and as a result we have been able to formulate a new approach to Indian affairs. Throughout this entire process, we have regularly consulted the opinions of the Indian people, and their views have played a major role in the formulation of Federal policy.

As we move ahead in this important work, it is essential that the Indian people continue to lead the way by participating in policy development to the greatest possible degree. In order to facilitate such participation, I am asking the Indian members of the National Council on Indian Opportunity to sponsor field hearings throughout the nation in order to establish continuing dialogue between the Executive branch of government and the Indian population of our country. I have asked the Vice President to see that the first round of field hearings are completed before October.

The recommendations of this Administration represent an historic step forward in Indian policy. We are proposing to break sharply with past approaches to Indian problems. In place of a long series of piecemeal reforms, we suggest a new and coherent strategy. In place of policies which simply call for more spending, we suggest policies which call for wiser spending. In place of policies which oscillate between the deadly extremes of forced termination and constant paternalism, we suggest a policy in which the Federal government and the Indian community play complementary roles.

But most importantly, we have turned from the question of *whether* the Federal government has a responsibility to Indians to the question of *how* that responsibility can best be fulfilled. We have concluded that the Indians will get better programs and that public monies will be more effectively expended if the people who are most affected by these programs are responsible for operating them.

The Indians of America need Federal assistance—this much has long been clear. What has not always been clear, however, is that the Federal government needs Indian energies and Indian leadership if its assistance is to be effective in improving the conditions of Indian life. It is a new and balanced relationship between the United States Government and the first Americans that is at the heart of our approach to Indian problems. And that is why we now approach these problems with new confidence that they will successfully be overcome.

"WE HAVE ENDURED. WE ARE INDIANS."

Pit River Indian Council, California, 1970

Even as the Nixon administration prepared the legislative program that would hasten self-determination for the Indians, proof came from many directions that the end of the Indians' travail was far from being in sight. Throughout 1970 Indians confronted white men in all parts of the country over Indian grievances and injustices done to tribes.

In New Mexico the Taos Pueblos struggled for possession of the seat of their religion, their sacred Blue Lake and its surrounding lands. Despite President Nixon's support of their right to the land, which the Indian Claims Commission had already adjudged to be theirs, Pueblo appeals were brushed aside by the Senate Subcommittee on Indian Affairs only a few days after the President had spoken, and another five months were required before the Pueblos finally won their fight. In Alaska the Native peoples still contested for their right to fair treatment in their land claims case, and in Nevada the Pyramid Lake Paiute continued their fight to regain the water that the Bureau of Reclamation was diverting away from their lowering lake to an irrigation project. Colville Indians in eastern Washington were resisting termination, and Wisconsin Chippewa were opposing the taking of some of their lands for a new national park.

In Littleton, Colorado, Indians occupied a Bureau of Indian Affairs building to protest gross discrimination on the part of local BIA officials against Indians. In Gallup, New Mexico, other Indians confronted whites over alleged discrimination and exploitation, and in South Dakota Sioux and other Indians vented their anger against the federal government by camping atop the giant faces at Mount Rushmore and asserting their "occupation" of the site. At Puget Sound, Indians tried to take possession of Fort Lawton, an abandoned military post, while others, in New York City, tried to plant themselves on Ellis Island in New York harbor, much as had been done at Alcatraz. Although both of these attempts failed, Indian militancy increased on both coasts. On Washington's Puyallup River, fury exploded in another clash between Indians defending their fishing rights and a small army of police and state officers, who threw tear gas, arrested sixty-three Indians and their supporters, and bulldozed the Indians' fishing camp. In upper New York State, Iroquois Indians battled in and out of court to eject whites from their reservation land.

Other Indians fought for their water rights along the Colorado River and against power plants polluting the air above reservations. In Michigan more than 250 Chippewa Indians, some wearing war paint and ceremonial clothes, laid claim to a lighthouse and acreage along Lake Superior; one of the Indian leaders announced angrily that "if the government doesn't start living up to its obligations, armed resistance and occupation will have to become a regular thing."

These manifestations of Red Power were a sign that the Indian pot was boiling, and the lid was rattling loudly. Indian desperation was no longer being repressed. One example of frustration no longer contained was provided by the 529 members of the Pit River Indian Tribe of northern California. In 1853, during the Gold Rush, their ancestors had been forcibly removed from their lands and placed on a reservation. In 1956 the Indian Claims Commission had agreed that the land had been taken illegally from the tribe and that the Indians should be paid by the federal government for some 3,368,000 acres that the Indians had never ceded. The tribe decided that it would not take money, but instead wanted the government to return the land, 90 per cent of which was then held either by government public land agencies like the Forest Service or by large corporations. Despite the Indians' stated position, the government offered the tribe forty-seven cents an acre in 1963. The Indians turned it down and continued their demand for the return of their land.

In 1970 their patience reached an end. On June 5, 150 members of the tribe tried to occupy a site in Lassen National Park, which they claimed still belonged to them, and were ejected by federal police. The following day another 150 Indians who had moved onto land held by the Pacific Gas and Electric Company were dispersed, and thirty-four Indians were arrested. Later that week seventeen more Indians were jailed for trespassing. As the conflict continued indecisively the Pit River Tribal Council, through its chairman, Mickey Gemmill, issued the following proclamation, a defiant pronouncement that reflects the frustrations and anger of Indians struggling against the overwhelming odds of the modern white society for the redress of wrongs committed against their peoples in the past and present.

TO THE PRESIDENT AND THE PEOPLE
OF THE UNITED STATES

In defiance of the treaties signed with Indian tribes in California and across the nation, the federal government is in the process of relinquishing its duties to the American Indian.

This process, called termination, has had a particularly

devastating effect on the Indians of California. To add to the injury, the state of California has not assumed its responsibilities promised to its Indian citizens, the original owners of the land.

Therefore it is up to the Indian people themselves to run their own affairs.

This will require that Indian people have the basic tools necessary to develop their communities, the tools and resources which have been taken by the white man.

The Pit River Indian Tribe has voted unanimously to refuse the payment under the California Land Claims Case now being prepared for settlement. We believe that money cannot buy the Mother Earth. She has sheltered and clothed, nourished and protected us. We have endured. We are Indians.

We are the rightful and legal owners of the land. Therefore, we reclaim all the resourceful land that has traditionally been ours, with the exception of that "owned" by private individuals.

On this land we will set up our own economic and social structure, retaining all the values that are commensurate with Indian life. We will encourage and help other Indian tribes and groups to establish similar structures across the country, in order to establish inter-tribal economics and cultural ties, basing the economy on the barter system.

Therefore let it be known by all concerned that the Pit River Tribe makes the following demands:

1. That the U.S. Government and the large corporations, including PG&E, PT&T, Southern Pacific Railroad, Kimberly Clark, Hearst Publications, and the Los Angeles Times-Mirror Corp., among others, return all our land to us immediately. No amount of money can buy the Mother Earth; therefore, the California Land Claims Case has no meaning. The Earth is our Mother, and we cannot sell her.

2. That the U.S. Government and the large corporations pay back to us the profits they have made from the land since 1853, and that they make an accounting to us immediately. The land was taken illegally, against the principles of the Constitution.

3. That reparations be made to all California Indians for the deaths, suffering, and poverty forced on Indians for over 100 years.

4. That the federal government and the large corporations undo the damage they have done to the land, and that they make reparations to us for the damage done. Where the forest has been cut away, it must be restored. Where the rivers have been dammed, they must be allowed to run freely.

5. That all Indians be allowed religious and cultural freedom, and be allowed to teach their children the Indian way of life and be proud of that life. Further, that Indian studies be instituted in schools around the country, so that all citizens will know the true story of the Indian. The stereotype of the Indian that exists must be erased.

These demands are inseparable, inter-related, and must all be carried out in full force together.

THIS COUNTRY WAS A LOT BETTER OFF WHEN THE INDIANS WERE RUNNING IT

by Vine Deloria, Jr.

The Native Americans, whom the white man long ago lumped together under the collective name "Indians," are many different peoples with different languages, physical characteristics, cultures, histories, and present-day needs, desires, and problems.

For these reasons, if for no other, no single Indian has yet emerged as a spokesman for all Indians. In his speeches and writings, however, Vine Deloria, Jr., a Standing Rock Sioux, has managed to articulate, with eloquence, wit, and anger, the attitudes, frustrations, and hopes of great numbers of Indians in every part of the country. A former executive director of the National Congress of American Indians, he is the author of the brilliant and biting *Custer Died for Your Sins*, published in 1969 when he was thirty-five years old, and of a second book, *We Talk, You Listen*.

The following article by him, a personal appraisal of the strengths and values that sustained the Indian peoples through dark days and continue to support them as they catch the "scent of victory in the air," appeared originally in *The New York Times* magazine on March 8, 1970.

O n Nov. 9, 1969, a contingent of American Indians, led by Adam Nordwall, a Chippewa from Minnesota, and Richard Oakes, a Mohawk from New York, landed on Alcatraz Island in San Francisco Bay and claimed the 13-acre rock "by right of discovery." The island had been abandoned six and a half years ago, and although there had been various suggestions concerning its disposal nothing had been done to make use of the land. Since there are Federal treaties giving some tribes the right to abandoned Federal property within a tribe's original territory, the Indians of the Bay area felt that they could lay claim to the island.

For nearly a year the United Bay Area Council of American Indians, a confederation of urban Indian organizations, had been talking about submitting a bid for the island to use it as a West Coast Indian cultural center and vocational training headquarters. Then, on Nov. 1, the San Francisco American Indian Center burned down. The center had served an estimated 30,000 Indians in the immediate area and was the focus of activities of the urban Indian community. It became a matter of urgency after that and, as Adam Nordwall said, "it was GO." Another landing, on Nov. 20, by nearly 100 Indians in a swift midnight raid secured the island.

The new inhabitants have made "the Rock" a focal point symbolic of Indian people. Under extreme difficulty they have worked to begin repairing sanitary facilities and buildings. The population has been largely transient, many people have stopped by, looked the situation over for a few days, then gone home, unwilling to put in the tedious work necessary to make the island support a viable community.

The Alcatraz news stories are somewhat shocking to non-Indians. It is difficult for most Americans to comprehend that there still exists a living community of nearly one million Indians in this country. For many people, Indians have become a species of movie actor periodically dispatched to the Happy Hunting Grounds by John Wayne on the "Late, Late Show." Yet there are some 315 Indian tribal groups in 26 states still functioning as quasi-sovereign nations under treaty status; they range from the mammoth Navajo tribe of some 132,000 with 16 million acres of land to tiny Mission Creek of California with 15 people and a tiny parcel of property. There are over half a million Indians in the cities alone, with the largest concentrations in San Francisco, Los Angeles, Minneapolis and Chicago.

The take-over of Alcatraz is to many Indian people a demonstration of pride in being Indian and a dignified, yet humorous protest against current conditions existing on the reservations and in the cities. It is this special pride and dignity, the determination to judge life according to one's own values, and the unconquerable conviction that the tribes will not die that has always characterized Indian people as I have known them.

I was born in Martin, a border town on the Pine Ridge Indian Reservation in South Dakota, in the midst of the Depression. My father was an Indian missionary who served 18 chapels on the eastern half of the reservation. In 1934, when I was 1, the Indian Reorganization Act was passed, allowing Indian tribes full rights of self-government for the first time since the late eighteen-sixties. Ever since those days, when the Sioux had agreed to forsake the life of the hunter for that of the farmer, they had been systematically deprived of any voice in decisions affecting their lives and property. Tribal ceremonies and religious practices were forbidden. The reservation was fully controlled by men in Washington, most of whom had never visited a reservation and felt no urge to do so.

The first years on the reservations were extremely hard for the Sioux. Kept confined behind fences they were almost wholly dependent upon Government rations for their food supply. Many died of hunger and malnutrition. Game was scarce and few were allowed to have weapons for fear of another Indian war. In some years there was practically no food available. Other years rations were withheld until the men agreed to farm the tiny pieces of land each family had been given. In desperation many families were forced to eat stray dogs and cats to keep alive.

By World War I, however, many of the Sioux families had developed prosperous ranches. Then the Government stepped in, sold the Indians' cattle for wartime needs, and after the war leased the grazing land to whites, creating wealthy white ranchers and destitute Indian landlords.

With the passage of the Indian Reorganization Act, native ceremonies and practices were given full recognition by Federal authorities. My earliest memories are of trips along dusty roads to Kyle, a small settlement in the heart of the reservation, to attend the dances. Ancient men, veterans of battles even then considered footnotes to the settlement of the West, brought their costumes out of hiding and walked about the grounds gathering the honors they had earned half a century before. They danced as if the intervening 50 years had been a lost weekend from which they had fully recovered. I remember best Dewey Beard, then in his late 80's and a survivor of the Little Big Horn. Even at that late date Dewey was hesitant to speak of the battle for fear of reprisal. There was no doubt, as one watched the people's expressions, that the Sioux had survived their greatest ordeal and were ready to face whatever the future might bring.

In those days the reservation was isolated and unsettled. Dirt roads held the few mail routes together. One could easily get lost in the wild back country as roads turned into cowpaths without so much as a backward glance. Remote settlements such as Buzzard Basin and Cuny Table were nearly inaccessible. In the spring every bridge on the reservation would be washed out with the first rain and would remain out until late summer. But few people cared. Most of the reservation people, traveling by team and wagon, merely forded the creeks and continued their journey, almost contemptuous of the need for roads and bridges.

The most memorable event of my early childhood was visiting Wounded Knee where 200 Sioux, including women and children, were slaughtered in 1890 by troopers of the Seventh Cavalry in what is believed to have been a delayed act of vengeance for Custer's defeat. The people were simply lined up and shot down much as was allegedly done, according to newspaper reports, at Songmy. The wounded were left to die in a three-day Dakota blizzard, and when the soldiers returned to the scene after the storm some were still alive and were saved. The massacre was vividly etched in the minds of many of the older reservation people, but it was difficult to find anyone who wanted to talk about it.

Many times, over the years, my father would point out survivors of the massacre, and people on the reservation always went out of their way to help them. For a long time there was a bill in Congress to pay indemnities to the survivors, but the War Department always insisted that it had been a "battle" to stamp out the Ghost Dance religion among the Sioux. This does not, however, explain bayoneted Indian women and children found miles from the scene of the incident.

Strangely enough, the Depression was good for Indian reservations, particularly for the people at Pine Ridge. Since their lands had been leased to non-Indians by the Bureau of Indian Affairs, they had only a small rent check and the contempt of those who leased their lands to show for their ownership. But the Federal programs devised to solve the national economic crisis were also made available to Indian people, and there was work available for the first time in the history of the reservations.

The Civilian Conservation Corps set up a camp on the reservation and many Indians were hired under the program. In the canyons north of Allen, S.D., a beautiful buffalo pasture was built by the C.C.C., and the whole area was transformed into a recreation wonderland. Indians would come from miles around to see the buffalo and leave with a strange look in their eyes. Many times I stood silently watching while old men talked to the buffalo about the old days. They would conclude by singing a song before respectfully departing, their eyes filled with tears and their minds occupied with the memories of other times and places. It was difficult to determine who was the captive—the buffalo fenced in or the Indian fenced out.

While the rest of America suffered from the temporary deprivation of its luxuries, Indian people had a period of prosperity, as it were. Paychecks were regular. Small cattle herds were started, cars were purchased, new clothes and necessities became available. To a people who had struggled along on $50 cash income per year, the C.C.C. was the greatest program ever to come along. The Sioux had climbed from absolute deprivation to mere poverty, and this was the best time the reservation ever had.

World War II ended this temporary prosperity. The C.C.C. camps were closed; reservation programs were cut to the bone and social services became virtually nonexistent; "Victory gardens" were suddenly the style, and people began to be aware that a great war was being waged overseas.

The war dispersed the reservation people as nothing ever had. Every day, it seemed, we would be bidding farewell to families as they headed west to work in the defense plants on the Coast.

A great number of Sioux people went west and many of the Sioux on Alcatraz today are their children and relatives. There may now be as many Sioux in California as there are on the reservations in South Dakota because of the great wartime migration.

Those who stayed on the reservation had the war brought directly to their doorstep when they were notified that their sons had to go across the seas and fight. Busloads of Sioux boys left the reservation for parts unknown. In many cases even the trip to nearby Martin was a new experience for them, let alone training in Texas, California or Colorado. There were always going-away ceremonies conducted by the older people who admonished the boys to uphold the old tribal traditions and not to fear death. It was not death they feared but living with an unknown people in a distant place.

I was always disappointed with the Government's way of handling Indian servicemen. Indians were simply lost in the shuffle of 3 million men in uniform. Many boys came home on furlough and feared to return. They were not cowards in any sense of the word but the loneliness and boredom of stateside duty was crushing their spirits. They spent months without seeing another Indian. If the Government had recruited all-Indian outfits it would have easily solved this problem and also had the best fighting units in the world at its disposal. I often wonder what an all-Sioux or Apache company, painted and singing its songs, would have done to the morale of élite German panzer units.

After the war Indian veterans straggled back to the reservations and tried to pick up their lives. It was very difficult for them to resume a life of poverty after having seen the affluent outside world. Some spent a few days with the old folks and then left again for the big cities. Over the years they have emerged as leaders of the urban Indian movement. Many of their children are the nationalists of today who are adamant about keeping the reservations they have visited only on vacations. Other veterans stayed on the reservations and entered tribal politics.

The reservations radically changed after the war. During the Depression there were about five telephones in Martin. If there was a call for you, the man at the hardware store had to come down to your house and get you to answer it. A couple of years after the war a complete dial system was installed that extended to most of the smaller communities on the reservation. Families that had been hundreds of miles from any form of communication were now only minutes away from a telephone.

Roads were built connecting the major communities of the Pine Ridge country. No longer did it take hours to go from one place to another. With these kinds of roads everyone had to have a car. The team and wagon vanished, except for those families who lived at various "camps" in inaccessible canyons pretty much as their ancestors had. (Today, even they have adopted the automobile for traveling long distances in search of work.)

I left the reservation in 1951 when my family moved to Iowa. I went back only once for an extended stay, in the summer of 1955, while on a furlough, and after that I visited only occasionally during summer vacations. In the meantime, I attended college, served a hitch in the Marines, and went to the seminary. After I graduated from the seminary, I took a job with the United Scholarship Service, a private organization devoted to the college and secondary-school education of American Indian and Mexican students. I had spent my last two years of high school in an Eastern preparatory school and so was probably the only Indian my age who knew what an independent Eastern school was like. As the program developed, we soon had some 30 students placed in Eastern schools.

I insisted that all the students who entered the program be able to qualify for scholarships as students and not simply as

Indians. I was pretty sure we could beat the white man at his own educational game, which seemed to me the only way to gain his respect. I was soon to find that this was a dangerous attitude to have. The very people who were supporting the program—non-Indians in the national church establishments—accused me of trying to form a colonialist "élite" by insisting that only kids with strong test scores and academic patterns be sent east to school. They wanted to continue the ancient pattern of soft-hearted paternalism toward Indians. I didn't feel we should cry our way into the schools; that sympathy would destroy the students we were trying to help.

In 1964, while attending the annual convention of the National Congress of American Indians, I was elected its executive director. I learned more about life in the N.C.A.I. in three years than I had in the previous 30. Every conceivable problem that could occur in an Indian society was suddenly thrust at me from 315 different directions. I discovered that I was one of the people who were supposed to solve the problems. The only trouble was that Indian people locally and on the national level were being played off one against the other by clever whites who had either ego or income at stake. While there were many feasible solutions, few could be tried without whites with vested interests working night and day to destroy the unity we were seeking on a national basis.

In the mid-nineteen-sixties, the whole generation that had grown up after World War II and had left the reservations during the fifties to get an education was returning to Indian life as "educated Indians." But we soon knew better. Tribal societies had existed for centuries without going outside themselves for education and information. Yet many of us thought that we would be able to improve the traditional tribal methods. We were wrong.

For three years we ran around the conference circuit attending numerous meetings called to "solve" the Indian problems. We listened to and spoke with anthropologists, historians, sociologists, psychologists, economists, educators and missionaries. We worked with many Government agencies and with every conceivable doctrine, idea and program ever created. At the end of this happy round of consultations the reservation people were still plodding along on their own time schedule, doing the things they considered important. They continued to solve their problems their way in spite of the advice given them by "Indian experts."

By 1967 there was a radical change in thinking on the part of many of us. Conferences were proving unproductive. Where non-Indians had been pushed out to make room for Indian people, they had wormed their way back into power and again controlled the major programs serving Indians. The poverty programs, reservation and university technical assistance groups were dominated by whites who had pushed Indian administrators aside.

Reservation people, meanwhile, were making steady progress in spite of the numerous setbacks suffered by the national Indian community. So, in large part, younger Indian leaders who had been playing the national conference field began working at the local level to build community movements from the ground up. By consolidating local organizations into power groups they felt that they would be in a better position to influence national thinking.

Robert Hunter, director of the Nevada Intertribal Council, had already begun to build a strong state organization of tribes and communities. In South Dakota, Gerald One Feather, Frank LaPointe and Ray Briggs formed the American Indian Leadership Conference, which quickly welded the educated young Sioux in that state into a strong regional organization active in nearly every phase of Sioux life. Gerald is now running for the prestigious post of Chairman of the Oglala Sioux, the largest Sioux tribe, numbering some 15,000 members. Ernie Stevens, an Oneida from Wisconsin and Lee Cook, a Chippewa from Minnesota, developed a strong program for economic and community development in Arizona. Just recently Ernie has moved into the post of director of the California Intertribal Council, a statewide organization representing some 130,000 California Indians in cities and on the scattered reservations of that state.

By the fall of 1967, it was apparent that the national Indian scene was collapsing in favor of strong regional organizations, although the major national organizations such as the National Congress of American Indians and the National Indian Youth Council continued to grow. There was yet another factor emerging on the Indian scene: the old-timers of the Depression days had educated a group of younger Indians in the old ways and these people were now becoming a major force in Indian life. Led by Thomas Banyaca of the Hopi, Mad Bear Anderson of the Tuscaroras, Clifton Hill of the Creeks, and Rolling Thunder of the Shoshones, the traditional Indians were forcing the whole Indian community to rethink its understanding of Indian life.

The message of the traditionalists is simple. They demand a return to basic Indian philosophy, establishment of ancient methods of government by open council instead of elected officials, a revival of Indian religions and replacement of white laws with Indian customs; in short, a complete return to the ways of the old people. In an age dominated by tribalizing communications media, their message makes a great deal of sense.

But in some areas their thinking is opposed to that of the National Congress of American Indians, which represents officially elected tribal governments organized under the Indian Reorganization Act as Federal corporations. The contemporary problem is therefore one of defining the meaning of "tribe." Is it a traditionally organized band of Indians following customs with medicine men and chiefs dominating the policies of the tribe, or is it a modern corporate structure attempting to compromise at least in part with modern white culture?

The problem has been complicated by private foundations' and Government agencies' funding of Indian programs. In general this process, although it has brought a great amount of money into Indian country, has been one of cooptation. Government agencies must justify their appropriation requests every year and can only take chances on spectacular programs that will serve as showcases of progress. They are not willing to invest the capital funds necessary to build viable self-sup-

porting communities on the reservations because these programs do not have an immediate publicity potential. Thus,
the Government agencies are forever committed to conducting conferences to discover that one "key" to Indian life that
will give them the edge over their rival agencies in the annual
appropriations derby.

Churches and foundations have merely purchased an Indian leader or program that conforms with their ideas of what
Indian people should be doing. The large foundations have
bought up the well-dressed, handsome "new image" Indian
who is comfortable in the big cities but virtually helpless at
an Indian meeting. Churches have given money to Indians
who have been willing to copy black militant activist tactics,
and the more violent and insulting the Indian can be, the more
the churches seem to love it. They are wallowing in self-guilt
and piety over the lot of the poor, yet funding demagogues of
their own choosing to speak for the poor.

I did not run for re-election as executive director of the
N.C.A.I. in the fall of 1967, but entered law school at the
University of Colorado instead. It was apparent to me that
the Indian revolution was well under way and that someone
had better get a legal education so that we could have our
own legal program for defense of Indian treaty rights. Thanks
to a Ford Foundation program, nearly 50 Indians are now in
law school, assuring the Indian community of legal talent in
the years ahead. Within four years I foresee another radical
shift in Indian leadership patterns as the growing local movements are affected by the new Indian lawyers.

There is an increasing scent of victory in the air in Indian
country these days. The mood is comparable to the old days
of the Depression when the men began to dance once again.
As the Indian movement gathers momentum and individual
Indians cast their lot with the tribe, it will become apparent
that not only will Indians survive the electronic world of Marshall McLuhan, they will thrive in it. At the present time
everyone is watching how mainstream America will handle
the issues of pollution, poverty, crime and racism when it does
not fundamentally understand the issues. Knowing the impor-

tance of tribal survival, Indian people are speaking more and more of sovereignty, of the great political technique of the open council, and of the need for gaining the community's consensus on all programs before putting them into effect.

One can watch this same issue emerge in white society as the "Woodstock Nation," the "Blackstone Nation" and the block organizations are developed. This is a full tribalizing process involving a nontribal people, and it is apparent that some people are frightened by it. But it is the kind of social phenomenon upon which Indians feast.

In 1965 I had a long conversation with an old Papago. I was trying to get the tribe to pay its dues to the National Congress of American Indians and I had asked him to speak to the tribal council for me. He said that he would but that the Papagos didn't really need the N.C.A.I. They were like, he told me, the old mountain in the distance. The Spanish had come and dominated them for 300 years and then left. The Mexicans had come and ruled them for a century, but they also left. "The Americans," he said, "have been here only about 80 years. They, too, will vanish but the Papagos and the mountain will always be here."

This attitude and understanding of life is what American society is searching for.

I wish the Government would give Alcatraz to the Indians now occupying it. They want to create five centers on the island. One center would be for a North American studies program; another would be a spiritual and medical center where Indian religions and medicines would be used and studied. A third center would concentrate on ecological studies based on an Indian view of nature—that man should live *with* the land and not simply *on* it. A job-training center and a museum would also be founded on the island. Certain of these programs would obviously require Federal assistance.

Some people may object to this approach, yet Health, Education and Welfare gave out $10-million last year to non-Indians to study Indians. Not one single dollar went to an Indian scholar or researcher to present the point of view of

Indian people. And the studies done by non-Indians added nothing to what was already known about Indians.

Indian people have managed to maintain a viable and cohesive social order in spite of everything the non-Indian society has thrown at them in an effort to break the tribal structure. At the same time, non-Indian society has created a monstrosity of a culture where people starve while the granaries are filled and the sun can never break through the smog.

By making Alcatraz an experimental Indian center operated and planned by Indian people, we would be given a chance to see what we could do toward developing answers to modern social problems. Ancient tribalism can be incorporated with modern technology in an urban setting. Perhaps we would not succeed in the effort, but the Government is spending billions every year and still the situation is rapidly growing worse. It just seems to a lot of Indians that this continent was a lot better off when we were running it.